SPELLING POWER

A Spelling Workbook with Comprehension Drills

Master the 320 Words Most Frequently Misspelled

Burton Goodman

 **Jamestown Publishers**

Providence, Rhode Island

 BURTON GOODMAN has taught English and reading in junior and senior high schools and in college for twenty years. He is the author of more than two dozen language arts texts, and his short stories, articles and adaptations have appeared in many national publications. He has written television and movie scripts for the Public Broadcasting System and Paramount Pictures. For four years he has served as Project Coordinator for the High School-College Continuum Program at the New York City Board of Education.

Spelling Power

A Spelling Workbook with Comprehension Drills

Catalog No. 150

©1987 by Burton Goodman

All rights reserved. The contents of this book are protected by the United States Copyright Law. Address all inquiries to Editor, Jamestown Publishers, Post Office Box 9168, Providence, Rhode Island 02940.

Cover and text design by Deborah Christie

Cover and text illustrations by Thomas Ewing Malloy

Printed in the United States of America

5 6 7 8 9 MU 98 97 96 95 94

ISBN 0-89061-449-0

Contents

To the Teacher	5
To the Student	7
Spelling Strategies	8
How to Complete a Lesson	9

Unit 1: Animal Crackers

Lesson 1	13
Lesson 2	15
Lesson 3	17
Lesson 4	19

Unit 2: People and Animals

Lesson 5	23
Lesson 6	25
Lesson 7	27
Lesson 8	29

Cumulative Review of Units 1 and 2	31

Unit 3: Food for Thought

Lesson 9	35
Lesson 10	37
Lesson 11	39
Lesson 12	41

Unit 4: Presenting the Presidents

Lesson 13	45
Lesson 14	47
Lesson 15	49
Lesson 16	51

Cumulative Review of Units 1-4	53

Unit 5: Literary Folk

Lesson 17	**57**
Lesson 18	**59**
Lesson 19	**61**
Lesson 20	**63**

Unit 6: Strange Stuff

Lesson 21	**67**
Lesson 22	**69**
Lesson 23	**71**
Lesson 24	**73**

Cumulative Review of Units 1-6 — **75**

Unit 7: Olympic Feats

Lesson 25	**79**
Lesson 26	**81**
Lesson 27	**83**
Lesson 28	**85**

Unit 8: Safety First

Lesson 29	**89**
Lesson 30	**91**
Lesson 31	**93**
Lesson 32	**95**

Cumulative Review of Units 1-8 — **97**

Answer Key — **99**

List of Words by Lessons — **103**

Alphabetical List of Words — *Inside Back Cover*

• To the Teacher •

This book has been specially designed to help your students master the 320 words most frequently misspelled by students, while simultaneously building their reading power.

There are thirty-six lessons and reviews—one for each week of the school year. (You may prefer to cover two lessons a week, to complete the material during a single term.) The book is organized into eight units, each containing four lessons. A Cumulative Review appears after every other unit.

Each lesson begins with a high-interest reading passage, which provides a context for the spelling words, as well as an opportunity for the students to develop their reading comprehension skills. Within each passage are ten boldfaced spelling words.

Each lesson begins on a right-hand page. Following the reading passage are five questions to help your students build their reading power in five important comprehension skills areas. The questions always appear in the same order. To increase reading POWER, students should

> **P**ick the main idea
> **O**bserve supporting details
> **W**atch for new vocabulary
> **E**xplain cause-and-effect relationships
> **R**ead between the lines: make inferences

Those questions provide your students with repeated practice in finding main ideas, recognizing details, deciphering the meanings of unfamiliar words from their context, understanding cause-and-effect relationships, and drawing inferences.

After the students have completed the Reading POWER portion of the lesson, they should write each of the ten boldfaced spelling words in a sentence in their notebooks. They should then be instructed to study the spelling of the words at home.

The way that students study spelling varies. There is no best way. Research has shown that different methods prove effective for different students. Here is a list of common methods of studying spelling:

- ▶ Look carefully at the word
- ▶ Write the word over and over
- ▶ Divide the word into its syllables
- ▶ Identify the difficult parts of the word and focus on them
- ▶ Find hints or clues in the word to help you remember its spelling
- ▶ Say the word, then spell it aloud
- ▶ Close your eyes and visualize the word

- Test yourself by covering the word and trying to spell it, then uncovering it to see if you are correct
- Have someone test you on the words
- Keep a list of the words you regularly misspell
- Review the words often

These methods are featured on page 8 for your students' use. Encourage the students to refer to that page, try each of the methods, and choose the ones that work best for them.

On the left-hand page of each lesson is a check of the students' mastery of most of the spelling words introduced in that lesson and of a few words from previous lessons. Your students should understand that after they have studied the spelling words in a particular lesson they should review all the words they have learned to that point. Explain to them that it is only through repeated study and review that they can expect to master the words.

The formats of the spelling checks vary. When you instruct the students to complete a Checking Your Spelling Power exercise, tell them that they should do so without looking back at the passage. You may have the students correct the exercises on their own, using the answer key in the back of the book, or you may wish to correct them as a class. Have students keep a list in their notebooks of the words that they misspell on the spelling checks. Tell them that they should give those words special attention when they study.

You may wish to periodically give oral tests of the words the students have studied. For your convenience, all the words introduced in the book are listed, by lesson number, on pages 103 and 104. A complete alphabetical list appears on the inside back cover.

Following the spelling check in each lesson is a section called Words Often Confused and Misused. It contains an explanation of the distinctions between two or three words that are commonly confused and misused, examples of their correct use, and an exercise that calls for the students to use the words. The students will be learning both the meanings and the spellings of those typically tangled words. They will be tested on those words in the Cumulative Reviews.

By carefully and conscientiously doing each lesson in SPELLING POWER, your students will master the 320 words most frequently misspelled by students, learn to spell and understand the meanings of 66 words that are often confused and misused, and at the same time quickly build their reading power. This program's special design will help them develop those skills steadily and surely.

The lessons are not hard, but the groups of spelling words introduced in each passage do increase slightly in difficulty as the book progresses. If your students do each lesson carefully and review every week, they will master the words and become better spellers for life.

•To the Student•

Are there certain words that you always misspell? Maybe you can't remember if you should change the *y* to *i,* or if a consonant should be doubled, or if it's *ie* or *ei*? Well, you're not alone. There is a long list of words that many people have trouble remembering how to spell. But you can learn to spell those words once and for all. Help is on the way in this book. It contains 320 words that people frequently misspell, and exercises to help you learn them. Through study and review, you can master those words and become a much better speller.

This book also contains 66 words that people commonly mix up and use incorrectly. Examples are *its* and *it's, accept* and *except,* and *stationary* and *stationery.* You will learn the differences in meaning between the words, as well as how to spell each one.

The program is not difficult. It simply requires effort and attention. If there's one key to success in spelling, it lies in the magic word *review.* By reviewing, over and over, you plant the words firmly in your mind. Without review, the words won't stick. After every eighth lesson, you will find a Cumulative Review. Each contains exercises to help you check how well you have learned the words that have been presented to that point in the book.

Last but not least, as you work your way through the book you will be increasing your reading comprehension. Each of the thirty-two lessons begins with a brief reading passage followed by five reading comprehension questions. The questions help you build your reading POWER by having you

> **P**ick the main idea
> **O**bserve supporting details
> **W**atch for new vocabulary
> **E**xplain cause-and-effect relationships
> **R**ead between the lines: make inferences

On the next two pages you will find a list of tried-and-true ways to study spelling, and directions on how to work your way through the lessons in the book. Look them both over carefully, and then you're on your way. Good luck!

Burton Goodman

Spelling Strategies

Here are some good ways to study spelling. Look them over, try them out, and pick the combination that is right for you!

▷ Look carefully at the word.

▷ Write the word over and over.

▷ Divide the word into its syllables.

▷ Identify the difficult parts of the word and focus your attention on them when studying. You might spell the word aloud, for instance, emphasizing the letters or letter combinations that give you difficulty. Or, you might underline the difficult parts of the word in your notebook.

▷ Find hints or clues in the word. For instance, there may be a little word or words within the word, which will help you remember the spelling. The word *separate,* for example, contains *"a rat."* Try to come up with other clues of your own in words that give you trouble.

▷ Say the word, then spell it aloud.

▷ Close your eyes and try to see the word in your mind.

▷ Test yourself by covering the word and trying to spell it, then uncovering it and checking to see if you are correct.

▷ Have someone test you on the words.

▷ Keep a list of the words you regularly misspell when studying, or that you have misspelled on spelling checks.

▷ Review all your spelling words often. (This step is a must for everyone who wants to be a good speller!)

•How to Complete a Lesson•

▷ Read the passage carefully

▷ Answer the five reading comprehension questions that follow the passage. Working with these questions will help you become a better reader.

▷ Check your answers to the reading comprehension questions, using the answer key at the back of the book.

▷ Look at and carefully study the ten boldfaced words in the passage. They are words that people often misspell. In your spelling notebook, write each of those words in a sentence. Underline the spelling word in each sentence.

▷ Study the spellings of the words at home. Be sure also to review all the words you worked with in previous lessons. Concentrate especially on words you spelled incorrectly on the spelling check in each lesson. It is only by reviewing the words again and again that you will really learn them.

▷ At your teacher's direction, complete the Checking Your Spelling Power section on the second page of the lesson. It contains most of the words from the reading passage in the lesson, and also a few words from previous lessons. Check yourself without looking back at the passage.

▷ Check your answers, using the answer key at the back of the book.

▷ In your notebook, write down the words you missed on the spelling check. (You should keep a running list of all the words you miss on the spelling checks in the book.) Study and review those words until you master them.

▷ Complete the fourth section of the lesson, which teaches you the difference between words that look or sound alike but that have different meanings. They are words that people often mix up and use incorrectly. You will learn the meanings of the words, as well as how to spell them. The answers to the exercise are in the answer key.

UNIT 1
Animal Crackers

When you have completed this unit, you will have mastered 40 of the words that are most frequently misspelled and 8 words that are commonly confused and misused.

•1•

It may **surprise** you to **discover** that a snake can swallow whole an animal two or three times as thick as its own head. It can do so because it is capable of **making** its jaws open extremely wide. It then grips its **victim** with needle-sharp teeth and gulps it down.

Snakes cannot move their eyelids. Their eyes are protected by transparent coverings. They also do not have ears. However, snakes are not **dependent** upon ears for hearing. They can **sense** sound by vibrations of the ground. Snakes are also skilled, or <u>proficient</u>, at tracking other animals. By **using** their tongues, they can **receive** an animal's scent. They then follow the scent. Snakes are **truly fascinating** animals.

Checking Your Reading Power

Put an *x* in the box before the correct answer to each question.

Main Idea
1. This selection is mainly about
   - ☐ a. how snakes eat.
   - ☐ b. how snakes sense movement.
   - ☐ c. why snakes are fascinating.

Supporting Details
2. Snakes do not have
   - ☐ a. bones.
   - ☐ b. ears.
   - ☐ c. tongues.

Vocabulary in Context
3. What is the meaning of the word <u>proficient</u>?
   - ☐ a. poor
   - ☐ b. skilled
   - ☐ c. difficult

Cause and Effect
4. A snake can tell that another creature is near by
   - ☐ a. sniffing its scent.
   - ☐ b. hearing its cries.
   - ☐ c. feeling the movement of the ground.

Inference
5. This passage suggests that snakes
   - ☐ a. fear larger animals.
   - ☐ b. are helpless.
   - ☐ c. differ greatly from most animals.

More Spelling Power to You

Look back over the boldfaced words in the passage. Pay close attention to how they are spelled. Then, in your notebook, write each word in a sentence and underline the spelling word.

At home, study the spellings of the underlined words. For some good spelling strategies, turn to page 8.

After you have studied the words, you will complete the spelling check on the next page. It contains all the words from this lesson. Be sure not to look back at the words in the passage when you complete the exercise.

Checking Your Spelling Power

Complete this exercise without looking back at the words. In each of the following rows of words, one of the words is misspelled. On the line to the left, write the letter of the misspelled word.

1. _____ a. dependent   b. surprise   c. trully
2. _____ a. victim   b. makeing   c. sense
3. _____ a. descover   b. using   c. receive
4. _____ a. surprise   b. fasinating   c. dependent
5. _____ a. sence   b. truly   c. victim
6. _____ a. useing   b. dependent   c. receive
7. _____ a. making   b. discover   c. suprise
8. _____ a. sense   b. recieve   c. truly
9. _____ a. fascinating   b. victem   c. making
10. _____ a. using   b. surprise   c. dependant

Check your answers in the answer key on page 99. In your notebook, keep a list of the words you misspelled. Study those words until you master them.

Words Often Confused and Misused

The words *accept* and *except* sound alike and have similar spellings. Therefore, they are often confused and misused. Carefully study the meanings of the words and the sample sentences. Then do the exercise that follows.

accept   The word *accept* is a verb. It means "to receive."

except   The word *except* is usually a preposition that means "but."

> With many thanks, I **accept** your electric potato peeler.
> Everyone **except** Pat is singing off key.
> I would **accept** the modesty award, **except** I don't deserve it.

Complete the sentences below by writing the words *accept* and *except* in the proper blanks.

1. I can _____ anything _____ criticism.
2. Everyone _____ Henry was willing to _____ my apology.
3. Please _____ this pass, which is good any day of the week _____ Friday.

14

•2•

The largest animal that has ever lived on our planet is still alive today. This enormous creature is the blue whale.

Found in oceans all over the world, the blue whale is **generally** twenty to thirty feet long at birth. It **usually** grows to about ninety feet, **although** some blue whales **approach** one hundred feet in length. Fully grown, a blue whale may **weigh** 350,000 pounds. That is about twice the magnitude of the **biggest** dinosaur on record.

Like all whales, the blue whale is a mammal. It is **equipped** with lungs and must **occasionally** surface for air. It can be **drowned** if it becomes trapped underwater without **sufficient** air.

Checking Your Reading Power

Put an *x* in the box before the correct answer to each question.

Main Idea
1. This selection is mainly about
   - ☐ a. where blue whales are found.
   - ☐ b. the biggest dinosaur on record.
   - ☐ c. the size of the blue whale.

Supporting Details
2. The blue whale is a
   - ☐ a. fish.
   - ☐ b. reptile.
   - ☐ c. mammal.

Vocabulary in Context
3. What is the meaning of the word magnitude?
   - ☐ a. size
   - ☐ b. color
   - ☐ c. ability

Cause and Effect
4. If a whale does not obtain air occasionally, it will
   - ☐ a. drown.
   - ☐ b. become trapped underwater.
   - ☐ c. use its lungs to produce air.

Inference
5. This passage suggests that
   - ☐ a. most blue whales are one hundred feet long.
   - ☐ b. a one hundred-foot whale would be rare.
   - ☐ c. whales are weak for their size.

More Spelling Power to You

Look back over the boldfaced words in the passage. Pay close attention to how they are spelled. Then, in your notebook, write each word in a sentence and underline the spelling word.

At home, study the spellings of the underlined words. For some good spelling strategies, turn to page 8.

After you have studied the words, you will complete the spelling check on the next page. It contains some words from the last lesson, as well as most of the words from this lesson. So be sure to review all the words you have learned so far before completing the exercise. Concentrate especially on the words you misspelled on the last spelling check.

Checking Your Spelling Power

Complete this exercise without looking back at the words. In each of the following pairs of words, one word is spelled incorrectly. Circle that word. Then write it correctly on the line to the left.

.... 1. receive
aproach

.... 2. ocasionally
using

.... 3. fascinating
drownd

.... 4. bigest
dependent

.... 5. trully
although

.... 6. sense
wiegh

.... 7. equipt
using

.... 8. discover
usualy

.... 9. sufficent
making

.... 10. generally
suprise

Check your answers in the answer key on page 99. In your notebook, keep a list of the words you misspelled. Study those words until you master them.

Words Often Confused and Misused

The words *loose* and *lose* are often confused and misused. Carefully study the meanings of the words and the sample sentences. Then do the exercise that follows.

loose The word *loose* means "not tight" or "free." Note that *loose* rhymes with *noose*.

lose The word *lose* means "to misplace—not have any longer." Note that *lose* rhymes with *shoes*.

When the lion got **loose**, we went indoors.
I would rather **lose** my fortune than my good name.
If you **lose** ten pounds, your clothing will be **loose**.

Complete the sentences below by writing the words *loose* and *lose* in the proper blanks.

1. A .... thread can cause you to .... a button.
2. If you continue to play with .... shoelaces, we may .... the game.
3. After the tiger got ...., it managed to .... its pursuers.

Now review the Words Often Confused and Misused from the last lesson. They will be included in the Cumulative Review following lesson 8.

•3•

Your sight **probably** is **all right** if you are "blind as a bat." That is because bats are not blind, though they may give that impression.

Scientists who have been **studying** bats have learned that bats employ a remarkable radarlike **system** that guides them at night. As the bat **flies** through the night sky, it repeatedly utters a short, high **shriek**. When the sound strikes an object, an echo bounces back. From the echo, the bat can tell the size and shape of the object. In that way, a bat can locate an insect in total darkness. The bat can then swoop **straight toward** it for food.

As the bat <u>emits</u> its high piercing sound, it turns its head from side to side. Perhaps the **awkward** twisting motion gives observers the idea that bats cannot see. However, the notion that bats are blind is **nonsense**.

Checking Your Reading Power

Put an *x* in the box before the correct answer to each question.

Main Idea
1. This passage is mainly about
   - ☐ a. how bats find their way at night.
   - ☐ b. ways in which scientists have been studying bats.
   - ☐ c. why bats cannot see well.

Supporting Details
2. A bat twists its head from side to side when it
   - ☐ a. swoops toward an insect.
   - ☐ b. shrieks.
   - ☐ c. is attempting to hide.

Vocabulary in Context
3. What is the meaning of the word <u>emits</u>?
   - ☐ a. utters
   - ☐ b. catches
   - ☐ c. believes

Cause and Effect
4. Bats use a kind of radar system to
   - ☐ a. help themselves fly.
   - ☐ b. locate and identify objects at night.
   - ☐ c. give the impression they are blind.

Inference
5. This passage suggests that bats
   - ☐ a. use their ears rather than their eyes to find their way at night.
   - ☐ b. have great difficulty in finding food in total darkness.
   - ☐ c. can see better than most animals.

More Spelling Power to You

Look back over the boldfaced words in the passage. Pay close attention to how they are spelled. Then, in your notebook, write each word in a sentence and underline the spelling word.

At home, study the spellings of the underlined words. For some good spelling strategies, turn to page 8.

After you have studied the words, you will complete the spelling check on the next page. It contains some words from previous lessons, as well as most of the words from this lesson. So be sure to review all the words you have learned so far in this book. Concentrate especially on the list of words you misspelled on previous spelling checks.

Checking Your Spelling Power

Complete this exercise without looking back at the words. In each of the following groups of words, one word is misspelled. Circle the misspelled word. Then write it correctly on the line to the left.

....	1. weigh	receive	shreik	sufficient
....	2. approach	truly	alright	although
....	3. akward	fascinating	using	equipped
....	4. surprise	making	sense	nonsence
....	5. probaly	drowned	victim	biggest
....	6. discover	flys	dependent	all right
....	7. studying	generaly	usually	occasionally
....	8. toward	awkward	systim	truly
....	9. straight	dependant	fascinating	all right
....	10. makeing	using	surprise	receive

Check your answers in the answer key on page 99. In your notebook, keep a list of the words you misspelled. Study those words until you master them.

Words Often Confused and Misused

Because they are pronounced the same, the words *threw* and *through* are frequently confused and misused. Carefully study the meanings of the words and the sample sentences. Then do the exercise that follows.

threw   The word *threw* means "hurled." It is a verb—the past tense of *throw*.

through   The word *through* is a preposition. It usually means "from end to end" or "into."

He **threw** a baseball with dazzling speed and remarkable control.
They rushed **through** the castle in search of an exit.
With a sudden twist, the horse **threw** its rider **through** the air.

Complete the sentences below by writing the words *threw* and *through* in the proper blanks.

1. To no one's surprise, Marie .... the basketball right .... the hoop.
2. Sam .... his scarf around his neck and marched fearlessly .... the crowd.
3. We carefully looked .... the book Harold .... at us.

Now review the Words Often Confused and Misused from previous lessons. They will be included in the Cumulative Review following lesson 8.

•4•

You may find it hard to stomach these facts about animals.

The crocodile, **believe** it or not, carries several pounds of small stones in its stomach. There is a simple **explanation** for this **unusual** fact. It is **impossible** for the crocodile to chew its food; it must swallow it whole. The stones, **therefore**, are <u>indispensable</u>, or **absolutely necessary**. They help the crocodile grind up the food so that it can be digested.

Speaking of stomachs, the next time you have a **terrible ache** in your stomach, be thankful you're not a hippopotamus, because you'd really be in pain. A hippo's stomach is ten feet long. Be **grateful**, too, that you're not a cow, for cows have four stomachs.

Checking Your Reading Power

Put an *x* in the box before the correct answer to each question.

Main Idea
1. This selection is mainly about
   - ☐ a. eating habits of the crocodile.
   - ☐ b. the number of stomachaches in animals.
   - ☐ c. the fact that animals have many different kinds of stomachs.

Supporting Details
2. How many stomachs do cows have?
   - ☐ a. four
   - ☐ b. ten
   - ☐ c. two

Vocabulary in Context
3. In the passage, <u>indispensable</u> means
   - ☐ a. absolutely necessary.
   - ☐ b. sometimes helpful.
   - ☐ c. not needed.

Cause and Effect
4. A crocodile uses the stones in its stomach to
   - ☐ a. swallow its food.
   - ☐ b. chew its food.
   - ☐ c. grind up its food.

Inference
5. This passage suggests that
   - ☐ a. crocodiles are born with stones in their stomachs.
   - ☐ b. human beings have better stomachs than other animals do.
   - ☐ c. animals' stomachs do not all work the same way.

More Spelling Power to You

Look back over the boldfaced words in the passage. Pay close attention to how they are spelled. Then, in your notebook, write each word in a sentence and underline the spelling word.

At home, study the spellings of the underlined words. For some good spelling strategies, turn to page 8.

After you have studied the words, you will complete the spelling check on the next page. It contains some words from previous lessons, as well as most of the words from this lesson. So be sure to review all the words you have learned so far in this book. Concentrate especially on the list of words you misspelled on previous spelling checks.

Checking Your Spelling Power

Complete this exercise without looking back at the words. Each of the sentences below contains one misspelled word. Underline the misspelled word. Then write it correctly on the line before the sentence.

.... 1. It is impossable to receive high marks without studying.

.... 2. There is probably a simple explaination for that unusual occurrence.

.... 3. The movie had a facinating plot, although the acting was terrible.

.... 4. I am truly gratefull to you for showing such good sense.

.... 5. Even though her ankle began to acke, Louise kept running straight toward the finish line.

.... 6. The spacecraft is dipendent upon the landing system it is carrying.

.... 7. The beast is occasionally dangerous; therfore you must approach it with care.

.... 8. It was absolutly the biggest surprise of her life.

.... 9. They beleive the victim drowned long before he was found by the rescue workers.

.... 10. On a biking trip, it is neccesary to be equipped with supplies that are lightweight.

Check your answers in the answer key on page 99. In your notebook, keep a list of the words you misspelled. Study those words until you master them.

Words Often Confused and Misused

The words *quiet* and *quite* are frequently confused and misused. Carefully study the meanings of the words and the sample sentences. Then do the exercise that follows.

>   **quiet** The word *quiet* means "not loud" or "calm."
>
>   **quite** The word *quite* means "very" or "completely."
>
>   A piercing scream shattered the **quiet** of the night.
>   The coach was **quite** satisfied with her team's play.
>   A leopard, gliding with **quiet** grace, is **quite** a moving sight.

Complete the sentences below by writing the words *quiet* and *quite* in the proper blanks.

1. Although Tim is very ...., he is .... popular.

2. I was .... amazed that you remained .... for so long.

3. On the wall hung a .... beautiful painting of a .... country scene.

Now review the Words Often Confused and Misused from previous lessons. They will be included in the Cumulative Review following lesson 8.

UNIT 2
People and Animals

When you have completed this unit, you will have mastered 80 of the words that are most frequently misspelled and 16 words that are commonly confused and misused.

• 5 •

Frank Buck is considered the world's most famous collector of wild animals. Buck circled the globe more than a dozen times, from his **beginning** expedition in 1911 **until** his last voyage in 1936. He was searching for live animals to take back to circuses and zoos.

How well did Buck **succeed** in his task? He was able to **acquire** five thousand monkeys and was **responsible** for capturing thousands of snakes. One of those was the largest king cobra ever found. In all, Buck managed to collect more than twenty-five thousand animals during his long and illustrious **career**.

The next time you are in a **library**, look for the book *Bring 'Em Back Alive*. That work, **written** in 1931, offers an **interesting** and vivid **description** of Buck's adventures.

○   Checking Your Reading Power   ○

Put an *x* in the box before the correct answer to each question.

Main Idea
1. This selection is mainly about
   - ☐ a. an interesting book.
   - ☐ b. kinds of wild animals.
   - ☐ c. Frank Buck, animal collector.

Supporting Details
2. *Bring 'Em Back Alive* was written in
   - ☐ a. 1911.
   - ☐ b. 1931.
   - ☐ c. 1936.

Vocabulary in Context
3. What is the meaning of the word illustrious?
   - ☐ a. sick
   - ☐ b. poor
   - ☐ c. famous

Cause and Effect
4. Buck journeyed around the world because he
   - ☐ a. was a person who just couldn't settle down.
   - ☐ b. had no real home.
   - ☐ c. was looking for live animals.

Inference
5. We may infer that Buck
   - ☐ a. knew very little about wild animals.
   - ☐ b. killed the animals he captured.
   - ☐ c. sometimes met with danger in his work.

○   More Spelling Power to You   ○

Look back over the boldfaced words in the passage. Pay close attention to how they are spelled. Then, in your notebook, write each word in a sentence and underline the spelling word.

At home, study the spellings of the underlined words. For some good spelling strategies, turn to page 8.

After you have studied the words, you will complete the spelling check on the next page. It contains some words from previous lessons, as well as most of the words from this lesson. So be sure to review all the words you have learned so far in this book. Concentrate especially on the list of words you misspelled on previous spelling checks.

Checking Your Spelling Power

Complete this exercise without looking back at the words. In each of the following groups of words, one of the words is misspelled. On the line to the left, write the letter of the misspelled word.

1. _____ a. truly   b. responsable   c. receive
2. _____ a. career   b. therefore   c. necesary
3. _____ a. libary   b. sense   c. ache
4. _____ a. grateful   b. intresting   c. although
5. _____ a. begining   b. weigh   c. impossible
6. _____ a. written   b. shreik   c. studying
7. _____ a. occasionally b. nonsense   c. untill
8. _____ a. suceed   b. fascinating   c. flies
9. _____ a. absolutely   b. discription   c. surprise
10. _____ a. discover   b. dependent   c. aquire

Check your answers in the answer key on page 99. In your notebook, keep a list of the words you misspelled. Study those words until you master them.

Words Often Confused and Misused

Few words in the English language are more commonly confused and misused than *its* and *it's*. Yet, it is easy to tell when to use each word. Carefully study the meanings of the words and the sample sentences. Then do the exercise that follows.

its The word *its* is a possessive pronoun. It shows possession or ownership. *Its* means "belonging to it."

it's The word *it's* is a contraction (shortened form) of *it is*. The apostrophe takes the place of the letter *i* in *is*. *It's* always means "it is."

The dog lowered **its** head, sniffed **its** bowl, and wagged **its** tail.
Dave says **it's** a good movie, but Beth says **it's** boring.
I think **it's** amazing how a cat always manages to land on **its** paws.

Complete the sentences below by writing the words *it's* and *its* in the proper blanks.

1. Of course _____ dangerous to be in a car that has lost _____ steering.
2. Remember, _____ not winning or losing that counts, _____ the way you play the game.
3. When a crowd rises to _____ feet and shouts, "Bravo," that means _____ delighted with the performance.

Now review the Words Often Confused and Misused from previous lessons. They will be included in the Cumulative Review following lesson 8.

•6•

Two brothers named Montgolfier launched the first air travelers.

It all started in 1782, when the Montgolfiers were **busy** working in their shop. They **accidentally** made a discovery that filled them with **excitement**. They learned that hot air has the power to make things rise.

It soon became the brothers' **ambition** to construct a **balloon** that could carry passengers into the air. The Montgolfiers conducted many experiments. They were **eventually** ready for the crucial test.

It **happened** in June 1783. The Montgolfiers filled a large balloon with hot air and set it free. It would be difficult to **describe** the brothers' joy and **relief** as they watched the balloon soar to a **height** of six thousand feet. Aboard were the first air travelers—a chicken, a duck, and a sheep.

Checking Your Reading Power

Put an *x* in the box before the correct answer to each question.

Main Idea
1. This selection is mainly about how
   - ☐ a. the Montgolfiers made an amazing discovery.
   - ☐ b. a balloon rose to a height of six thousand feet.
   - ☐ c. three animals became the first air travelers.

Supporting Details
2. The Montgolfiers' successful balloon flight took place in
   - ☐ a. 1782.
   - ☐ b. 1783.
   - ☐ c. 1784.

Vocabulary in Context
3. What is the meaning of the word crucial as it is used in the passage?
   - ☐ a. first
   - ☐ b. most dangerous
   - ☐ c. most important

Cause and Effect
4. When they discovered that hot air could make things rise, the Montgolfiers
   - ☐ a. were filled with relief.
   - ☐ b. decided to build a balloon.
   - ☐ c. became the first air travelers.

Inference
5. The Montgolfiers probably selected animals to be the balloon's first passengers because
   - ☐ a. the Montgolfiers loved animals.
   - ☐ b. animals are lighter than people.
   - ☐ c. the Montgolfiers thought it was too dangerous to send a human being.

More Spelling Power to You

Look back over the boldfaced words in the passage. Pay close attention to how they are spelled. Then, in your notebook, write each word in a sentence and underline the spelling word.

At home, study the spellings of the underlined words. For some good spelling strategies, turn to page 8.

After you have studied the words, you will complete the spelling check on the next page. It contains some words from previous lessons, as well as most of the words from this lesson. So be sure to review all the words you have learned so far in this book. Concentrate especially on the list of words you misspelled on previous spelling checks.

Checking Your Spelling Power

Complete this exercise without looking back at the words. In each of the following pairs of words, one word is spelled incorrectly. Circle that word. Then write it correctly on the line to the left.

.... 1. succeed
　　　　　　　　　discribe

.... 2. writen
　　　　　　　　　busy

.... 3. until
　　　　　　　　　baloon

.... 4. recieve
　　　　　　　　　happened

.... 5. accidentaly
　　　　　　　　　straight

.... 6. beginning
　　　　　　　　　releif

.... 7. responsible
　　　　　　　　　excitment

.... 8. height
　　　　　　　　　usualy

.... 9. eventualy
　　　　　　　　　interesting

.... 10. alright
　　　　　　　　　ambition

Check your answers in the answer key on page 99. In your notebook, keep a list of the words you misspelled. Study those words until you master them.

Words Often Confused and Misused

The words *weather* and *whether* are often confused and misused. Carefully study the meanings of the words and the sample sentences. Then do the exercise that follows.

weather　The word *weather* refers to the climate or the condition of the air.

whether　The word *whether* is a conjunction that often means "if."

　　　　　I listen to the **weather** report every day.
　　　　　Mrs. Lee asked Frank **whether** he wanted to join the Science Club.
　　　　　We are going on vacation **whether** the **weather** is good or bad.

Complete the sentences below by writing the words *weather* and *whether* in the proper blanks.

1. Amy didn't know .... or not to take an umbrella, because the .... report said there was a slight chance of rain.

2. Although Mr. Cooper enjoys the .... in Maine, he can't decide .... to accept a job there or not.

3. According to the umpire, ... or not the game will be played depends upon the ....

Now review the Words Often Confused and Misused from previous lessons. They will be included in the Cumulative Review following lesson 8.

26

•7•

It was a long and difficult journey—1,135 miles through two mountain **ranges** and **across** the Yukon River. But when it was completed, Libby Riddle had reason to **celebrate**. She had won Alaska's Thirteenth Annual Anchorage-to-Nome Dogsled Race.

The most trying part of the three-week race was the struggle **against** abominable weather. Snow kept **coming** down **continually**, and a blizzard made it hard to see. But Libby managed to **conquer** the elements and keep moving **forward**.

According to the winner, most of the credit for her victory should go to the fifteen **courageous** dogs that pulled the sled. In **preparation** for the journey, Libby selected the healthiest and best dogs she could find to **accompany** her. Now she wishes she could share the $50,000 first prize with them.

○ Checking Your Reading Power ○

Put an *x* in the box before the correct answer to each question.

Main Idea
1. This selection is mainly about
   ☐ a. the distance from Anchorage to Nome.
   ☐ b. how to conquer the elements.
   ☐ c. a dogsled race in Alaska.

Supporting Details
2. How long did the trip take?
   ☐ a. two weeks
   ☐ b. three weeks
   ☐ c. fifteen weeks

Vocabulary in Context
3. What is the meaning of the word abominable?
   ☐ a. very unpleasant or miserable
   ☐ b. enjoyable or delightful
   ☐ c. having to do with the abdomen or stomach

Cause and Effect
4. In part, Libby Riddle's victory was due to the
   ☐ a. efforts of her courageous dogs.
   ☐ b. unusually fine weather.
   ☐ c. fact that the journey was long and difficult.

Inference
5. This passage suggests that Libby Riddle
   ☐ a. won the race through sheer luck.
   ☐ b. did not prepare well for the race.
   ☐ c. had both strength and determination.

○ More Spelling Power to You ○

Look back over the boldfaced words in the passage. Pay close attention to how they are spelled. Then, in your notebook, write each word in a sentence and underline the spelling word.

At home, study the spellings of the underlined words. For some good spelling strategies, turn to page 8.

After you have studied the words, you will complete the spelling check on the next page. It contains some words from previous lessons, as well as most of the words from this lesson. So be sure to review all the words you have learned so far in this book. Concentrate especially on the list of words you misspelled on previous spelling checks.

Checking Your Spelling Power

Complete this exercise without looking back at the words. In each of the following groups of words, one word is misspelled. Circle the misspelled word. Then write it correctly on the line to the left.

....	1. accidentally	eventually	continualy	generally
....	2. accross	equipped	approach	necessary
....	3. making	coming	useing	biggest
....	4. conquor	discover	therefore	awkward
....	5. ache	straight	dependent	foward
....	6. absolutely	couragous	interesting	grateful
....	7. celabrate	believe	impossible	terrible
....	8. describe	discover	preperation	busy
....	9. acompany	balloon	truly	written
....	10. acquire	career	against	ocasionally

Check your answers in the answer key on page 99. In your notebook, keep a list of the words you misspelled. Study those words until you master them.

Words Often Confused and Misused

The words *all ready* and *already* are commonly confused and misused. Carefully study the meanings of the words and the sample sentences. Then do the exercise that follows.

all ready The words *all ready* mean "all prepared" or "all set."

already The word *already* means "previously" or "earlier."

> The musicians were **all ready** to play.
> Raymond has **already** seen that play three times.
> We were **all ready** to go to the airport, when we learned that the plane had **already** arrived.

Complete the sentences below by writing *all ready* and *already* in the proper blanks.

1. Although we have .... played their team twice, we are .... to play them again.
2. The buses are .... to leave; in fact one bus has .... left.
3. The police have .... been called, and they are .... to make the arrest.

Now review the Words Often Confused and Misused from previous lessons. They will be included in the Cumulative Review following lesson 8.

• 8 •

Miami's MetroZoo was **losing** money, when someone thought of a **brilliant** way to increase **attendance**.

Visitors to the zoo were treated to an added attraction: a new specimen wearing a dark **business** suit, a white shirt, and a tie. It roamed around its pen doing such **familiar** things as shaving, brushing its teeth, watching television, and reading a newspaper. On **occasion**, it ate a meal offered by its keeper. Although the creature refused to **speak** to the patrons that regularly gathered around its pen, it willingly shook hands with them.

This **extraordinary exhibit** is one you are likely to **recognize**. It is known as "Urban Man."

Checking Your Reading Power

Put an *x* in the box before the correct answer to each question.

Main Idea
1. This selection is mainly about
   - ☐ a. visitors to the Miami MetroZoo.
   - ☐ b. an unusual exhibit at a zoo.
   - ☐ c. why a zoo was losing money.

Supporting Details
2. The specimen refused to
   - ☐ a. shake hands with visitors.
   - ☐ b. talk to zoo visitors.
   - ☐ c. read a newspaper.

Vocabulary in Context
3. As used in this selection, the word patrons means
   - ☐ a. paying visitors.
   - ☐ b. friends or neighbors.
   - ☐ c. specimens or examples.

Cause and Effect
4. The new specimen was added to the zoo in order to
   - ☐ a. increase attendance.
   - ☐ b. show people what "Urban Man" looks like.
   - ☐ c. hand out information about the zoo.

Inference
5. The new exhibit probably resulted in
   - ☐ a. anger rather than amusement on the part of most visitors.
   - ☐ b. decreased attendance at the zoo.
   - ☐ c. increased publicity about the zoo.

More Spelling Power to You

Look back over the boldfaced words in the passage. Pay close attention to how they are spelled. Then, in your notebook, write each word in a sentence and underline the spelling word.

At home, study the spellings of the underlined words. For some good spelling strategies, turn to page 8.

After you have studied the words, you will complete the spelling check on the next page. It contains some words from previous lessons, as well as most of the words from this lesson. So be sure to review all the words you have learned so far in this book. Concentrate especially on the list of words you misspelled on previous spelling checks.

Checking Your Spelling Power

Complete this exercise without looking back at the words. Each of the sentences below contains one misspelled word. Underline the misspelled word. Then write it correctly on the line before the sentence.

.... 1. He had perfect attendence from the beginning of the year until now.

.... 2. It was a brilliant plan, although it failed to suceed.

.... 3. I could hardly describe my excitement and relief at finally hearing a familar voice.

.... 4. Look in the library for *The Call of the Wild,* the extraordnary tale of a courageous dog.

.... 5. Gene has grown so much in height that it's almost impossible to reconize him.

.... 6. I am never too busy to celebrate a truly happy ocassion.

.... 7. The *Titanic* eventually sank, after the ship accidentally smashed into an iceberg and began loseing its power.

.... 8. In preparation for his new career, Phil planned to acquire some busness skills.

.... 9. The director called across the room, "It is necessary for you to speek much louder if you want to be absolutely certain of being heard."

.... 10. The jury bent forward to see exibit A—a letter written by the victim.

Check your answers in the answer key on page 99. In your notebook, keep a list of the words you misspelled. Study those words until you master them.

Words Often Confused and Misused

The words *whose* and *who's* are frequently confused and misused. Like *its* and *it's,* one word shows possession while the other is a contraction. Carefully study the meanings of the words and the sample sentences. Then do the exercise that follows.

whose   The word *whose* is a possessive adjective or pronoun meaning "of whom" or "of which."

who's   The word *who's* is a contraction. It means "who is" or "who has." The apostrophe takes the place of the missing letter or letters.

    I wonder **whose** book this is.
    That's Margaret, **who's** the best chess player in school.
    Whose house is the party at, and **who's** going to be there?

Complete the sentences below by writing the words *whose* and *who's* in the proper blanks.

1. I don't know .... idea it was, but Harry's the one .... taking credit.

2. Leslie, ... painting won first prize, is the girl .... standing near the door.

3. Anyone .... played soccer before should talk to Mr. Larsen, ... team needs players.

Now review the Words Often Confused and Misused from lessons 1–8. They will be included in the Cumulative Review that begins on the next page.

Cumulative Review of Units 1 and 2

I. In each of the following groups of words, one word is misspelled. Circle the misspelled word. Then write the word correctly on the line to the left.

1. alright
   busy
   happened

2. although
   probably
   equipt

3. sufficient
   eventualy
   ache

4. responsible
   recognize
   foward

5. against
   drownd
   celebrate

6. aproach
   exhibit
   beginning

7. bussiness
   describe
   system

8. therefore
   generaly
   continually

9. acidentally
   accompany
   making

10. sense
    awkward
    nonsence

II. Fill in the blanks in the words to create words that are spelled correctly. Then write the words on the lines to the left.

1. terr_ble
2. d_scover
3. attend_nce
4. prep_ration
5. conqu_r
6. spe_k
7. imposs_ble
8. r_sponsible
9. d_pend_nt
10. d_scr_ption

III. The letters *ie* or *ei* are missing from each of the words below. Fill in the blanks in each word to spell the word correctly. Then write the word on the line to the left.

1. rec__ve
2. h__ght
3. rel__f
4. shr__k
5. bel__ve

IV. In each of the following sentences, one of the three underlined words is misspelled. Circle the misspelled word. Then write the word correctly on the line before the sentence.

1. Our <u>libary</u> is <u>usually</u> open <u>until</u> nine o'clock on Thursday.

2. We are <u>certain</u> you will <u>succeed</u> in your <u>fasinating</u> new career.

3. There was <u>excitment</u> in the air as the <u>balloon</u> slowly started <u>coming</u> down.

4. *The Diary of a Young Girl* is one of the most interisting and extraordinary books ever written.

5. Everyone agreed it was truly a thoughtful and unusual suprise.

6. It is Joan's ambition to aquire the biggest collection of baseball cards in the world.

7. Is that Paul skating straiht across the rink toward us?

8. It is absolutely neccessary for me to spend more time studying.

9. Are you familiar with the explanation of how an airplane flys?

10. On this occassion, let us show you how grateful we are to you for your courageous deed.

V • Each of the following sentences contains two words in parentheses. Underline the one that makes the sentence correct. Then write the word on the line to the left.

1. Only the *drip, drip, drip* of a faucet broke the (quiet, quite).

2. Good (weather, whether) always seems to lift everyone's spirits.

3. Time flies—we're (all ready, already) doing this cumulative review.

4. The injured bird kept trying to flap (its, it's) wing.

5. Finally the sun broke (threw, through) the clouds.

6. Can you tell me (whose, who's) in charge here?

7. Since it is raining, I'll gladly (accept, except) your offer of a ride home.

8. Did anyone (loose, lose) a quarter with George Washington's face on it?

9. The room became (quiet, quite) cold after the furnace broke down.

10. The juggler (threw, through) one orange after another into the air.

11. I wonder if (its, it's) true that an elephant never forgets.

12. No matter how many times he was tied up, the great Houdini always managed to get (loose, lose).

13. Karen loves every season (accept, except) winter.

14. José is the student (whose, who's) poetry has won awards.

15. We couldn't decide (weather, whether) the glass was half empty or half full.

UNIT 3
Food For Thought

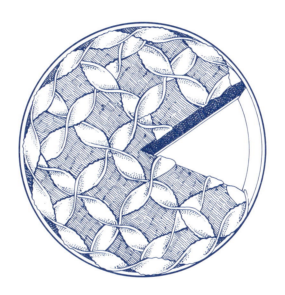

When you have completed this unit, you will have mastered 120 of the words that are most frequently misspelled and 25 words that are commonly confused and misused.

• 9 •

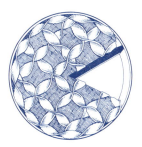

Do you appreciate salt? Chances are you see and use it so **often** that you take it for granted. But there are more than ten thousand uses for salt, and it has **always** held a place of **importance** in daily life.

At one time salt was so **valuable** and rare that it was used as money. In fact, the word *salary* comes from the word *salt*. During early Roman times, each **soldier** in Julius Caesar's army was **paid** a portion of his earnings in salt. That **quantity** was known as his *salarium*—or **salary**.

The term "not worth his salt" has a **similar** derivation, or origin. It is an expression of **criticism**. Someone who is "not worth his salt" is not worth his pay.

Checking Your Reading Power

Put an *x* in the box before the correct answer to each question.

Main Idea
1. This selection is mainly about
   - ☐ a. the ten thousand uses of salt.
   - ☐ b. the value of salt.
   - ☐ c. the derivation of the word *salary*.

Supporting Details
2. Through the years, salt has
   - ☐ a. had little value.
   - ☐ b. always been important.
   - ☐ c. always been easy to obtain.

Vocabulary in Context
3. What is the meaning of the word derivation?
   - ☐ a. goal
   - ☐ b. meaning
   - ☐ c. origin

Cause and Effect
4. Salt was once used as money because it was
   - ☐ a. rare and valuable.
   - ☐ b. easy to count.
   - ☐ c. very tasty.

Inference
5. Someone who is "worth her salt" is probably
   - ☐ a. lazy.
   - ☐ b. a good worker.
   - ☐ c. being paid too much.

More Spelling Power to You

Look back over the boldfaced words in the passage. Pay close attention to how they are spelled. Then, in your notebook, write each word in a sentence and underline the spelling word.

At home, study the spellings of the underlined words. For some good spelling strategies, turn to page 8.

After you have studied the words, you will complete the spelling check on the next page. It contains some words from previous lessons, as well as most of the words from this lesson. So be sure to review all the words you have learned so far in this book. Concentrate especially on the list of words you misspelled on previous spelling checks.

Checking Your Spelling Power

Complete this exercise without looking back at the words. In each of the following groups of words, one of the words is misspelled. On the line to the left, write the letter of the misspelled word.

1. _____ a. occasionally   b. truly   c. ofen
2. _____ a. similar   b. although   c. flys
3. _____ a. responsible   b. salery   c. beginning
4. _____ a. payed   b. receive   c. describe
5. _____ a. interesting   b. explenation   c. valuable
6. _____ a. balloon   b. weigh   c. criticicm
7. _____ a. quantity   b. straigt   c. until
8. _____ a. agenst   b. always   c. acquire
9. _____ a. importence   b. written   c. therefore
10. _____ a. accompany   b. ambishion   c. soldier

Check your answers in the answer key on page 100. In your notebook, keep a list of the words you misspelled. Study those words until you master them.

Words Often Confused and Misused

The words *to, too* and *two* are among the most commonly confused and misused words in the English language. However, you can easily learn when to use each word. Carefully study the meanings of the words and the sample sentences. Then do the exercise that follows.

to   The word *to* is usually a preposition that means "in the direction of." Sometimes *to* is used as part of a verb, as in *to speak*.

too The word *too* means "very," "also," or "more than enough."

two The word *two* refers to the number 2.

> Linda is planning **to** go **to** the department store **to** buy a notebook **to** take **to** school.
> Someone once said that we grow old **too** soon and wise **too** late; I believe that **too**.
> The **two** front tires need **two** pounds of air.
> After Dan ate **two** sandwiches, he was **too** full **to** move.

Complete the sentences below by writing *to, too* and *two* in the proper blanks.

1. If you go _____ the supermarket, _____, please purchase _____ grapefruits and some apples.

2. In order _____ get _____ my uncle's house, you must take _____ buses and a subway _____.

3. Do you think it is _____ late for us _____ hurry _____ the box office _____ buy _____ tickets?

Now review the Words Often Confused and Misused from previous lessons. They will be included in the Cumulative Review following lesson 16.

• 10 •

Every day, more than **forty million** Americans enjoy a hamburger or a **sandwich**. Surprisingly, these popular "American" foods originated in other countries.

You may have **guessed** that the **source** of the hamburger's name was the city of Hamburg, in Germany. Actually, however, the hamburger originated in Russia, where it was eaten raw. German sailors later took the recipe back to Hamburg. The natives there, however, found eating raw meat **disagreeable**. They decided to broil it. The result was the hamburger.

As for the sandwich, England's fourth Earl of Sandwich was playing cards when he began to get hungry. The earl was reluctant to **interrupt** his game, yet was **anxious** to eat. He solved his dilemma by instructing a servant to bring him a piece of roast beef between two slices of bread. That **permitted** the earl to eat with one hand and play cards with the other. And so the sandwich, which still bears the earl's name, came into **existence**.

Checking Your Reading Power

Put an *x* in the box before the correct answer to each question.

Main Idea
1. This selection is mainly about
   ☐ a. how German sailors brought a recipe to Hamburg.
   ☐ b. England's fourth Earl of Sandwich.
   ☐ c. how the hamburger and the sandwich originated.

Supporting Details
2. Raw hamburgers were first eaten in
   ☐ a. Germany.
   ☐ b. Russia.
   ☐ c. England.

Vocabulary in Context
3. What is the meaning of the word dilemma?
   ☐ a. problem
   ☐ b. anxiety
   ☐ c. hunger

Cause and Effect
4. The sandwich was invented as a result of
   ☐ a. the imagination of a clever servant.
   ☐ b. an earl's desire to both eat and play cards.
   ☐ c. a very interesting card game.

Inference
5. This passage suggests that foods
   ☐ a. usually come into being for odd reasons.
   ☐ b. are sometimes named for their origins.
   ☐ c. travel quickly from one place to another.

More Spelling Power to You

Look back over the boldfaced words in the passage. Pay close attention to how they are spelled. Then, in your notebook, write each word in a sentence and underline the spelling word.

At home, study the spellings of the underlined words. For some good spelling strategies, turn to page 8.

After you have studied the words, you will complete the spelling check on the next page. It contains some words from previous lessons, as well as most of the words from this lesson. So be sure to review all the words you have learned so far in this book. Concentrate especially on the list of words you misspelled on previous spelling checks.

Checking Your Spelling Power

Complete this exercise without looking back at the words. In each of the following pairs of words, one word is spelled incorrectly. Circle that word. Then write it correctly on the line to the left.

.... 1. sandwich
 allways

.... 2. fourty
 exhibit

.... 3. akward
 guessed

.... 4. million
 succed

.... 5. source
 extrordinary

.... 6. existance
 conquer

.... 7. library
 interupt

.... 8. permited
 business

.... 9. anxious
 valuble

.... 10. courageous
 disagreable

Check your answers in the answer key on page 100. In your notebook, keep a list of the words you misspelled. Study those words until you master them.

Words Often Confused and Misused

The words *than* and *then* are often confused and misused. As you will see, each has a very different meaning. Carefully study the meanings of the words and the sample sentences. Then do the exercise that follows.

than The word *than* is a conjunction or a preposition used in comparisons.

then The word *then* is usually an adverb or a noun that means "at that time."

>Mount McKinley is higher **than** Mount Logan, but Mount Everest is higher **than** Mount McKinley.
>The meeting is at four o'clock; I'll see you **then**.
>**Then** Mr. Grant asked if Ken was taller **than** his brother.

Complete the sentences below by writing *than* and *then* in the proper blanks.

1. I like fall better .... spring because Thanksgiving comes ....

2. Eleanor hurt her ankle when she stumbled; .... she began running slower

   .... usual.

3. When my grandfather talks about "the good old days," he says that prices ....

   were much lower .... they are today.

Now review the Words Often Confused and Misused from previous lessons. They will be included in the Cumulative Review following lesson 16.

•11•

Because of the expression "as American as apple pie," you might **naturally suppose** that apple pie is native to the United States. Like the hamburger and the sandwich, however, apple pie was invented in a foreign land. The French brought it to North America centuries ago.

Pies of all kinds have been popular in Europe for more than a thousand years. The ancient Romans, for example, loved to eat pies filled with meat, fish, or fowl. Strange as it sounds, a pie made with live birds was a special **banquet** dish.

The expression "as American as apple pie" probably developed because of the **genuine** ardor exhibited **among** Americans for apple pie. Surveys show that they **prefer** it by far to any other dessert. So the next time you order apple pie in a **restaurant** or **cafeteria**, be aware that you are **having** the U.S.'s **favorite** dessert.

Checking Your Reading Power

Put an *x* in the box before the correct answer to each question.

Main Idea
1. This selection is mainly about
   ☐ a. how the French brought apple pie to North America.
   ☐ b. the history of pie.
   ☐ c. apple pie as the favorite dessert in the United States.

Supporting Details
2. Pies made of live birds were once served by
   ☐ a. ancient Romans.
   ☐ b. early Americans.
   ☐ c. the French, centuries ago.

Vocabulary in Context
3. From the context of the paragraph in which the word appears, you can tell that ardor means
   ☐ a. patriotism.
   ☐ b. belief.
   ☐ c. enthusiasm.

Cause and Effect
4. It is likely that the expression "as American as apple pie" came about due to the
   ☐ a. fact that apple pie is native to the United States.
   ☐ b. popularity of apple pie in America.
   ☐ c. result of a survey of Americans.

Inference
5. This passage suggests that pies are
   ☐ a. an old food rather than a new one.
   ☐ b. not enjoyed very much in Europe.
   ☐ c. the most popular type of dessert the world over.

More Spelling Power to You

Look back over the boldfaced words in the passage. Pay close attention to how they are spelled. Then, in your notebook, write each word in a sentence and underline the spelling word.

At home, study the spellings of the underlined words. For some good spelling strategies, turn to page 8.

After you have studied the words, you will complete the spelling check on the next page. It contains some words from previous lessons, as well as most of the words from this lesson. So be sure to review all the words you have learned so far in this book. Concentrate especially on the list of words you misspelled on previous spelling checks.

Checking Your Spelling Power

Complete this exercise without looking back at the words. In each of the following groups of words, one word is misspelled. Circle the misspelled word. Then write it correctly on the line to the left.

....	1.	importance	cafeteria	often	using
....	2.	haveing	usually	forty	victim
....	3.	among	biggest	dependent	similiar
....	4.	paid	shriek	sandwitch	probably
....	5.	necessary	preferr	grateful	genuine
....	6.	interrupt	system	written	naturaly
....	7.	suppose	milion	existence	impossible
....	8.	disagreeable	excitement	restarant	brilliant
....	9.	weight	career	favrite	description
....	10.	banquit	accidentally	permitted	recognize

Check your answers in the answer key on page 100. In your notebook, keep a list of the words you misspelled. Study those words until you master them.

Words Often Confused and Misused

The words *weak* and *week* are frequently confused and misused. Study these words carefully. Then do the exercise that follows.

weak The word *weak* means "feeble or lacking strength."

week The word *week* means "seven days, one after another."

The old horse seemed too **weak** to pull the carriage.
Let's make plans to go to the museum next **week** or the following **week**.
The **week** after she had the flu, Liz still felt tired and **weak**.

Complete the sentences below by writing *weak* and *week* in the proper blanks.

1. Although Simon is sometimes a .... batter, he certainly hit the ball well last ....

2. At the beginning of the .... , Wayne's composition was poorly organized and .... ; by the end of the .... , it was outstanding.

3. The doctor said, "If you still feel .... in a .... , make an appointment to see me.

Now review the Words Often Confused and Misused from previous lessons. They will be included in the Cumulative Review following lesson 16.

•12•

What makes popcorn pop? Unlike **ordinary** corn, popcorn is composed of **extremely** hard kernels that have waterproof shells. As a kernel is heated, the moisture inside it turns to steam. When the **temperature** rises **enough**, the steam explodes the kernel, causing a *pop!* to **occur**.

Popping popcorn is fun, but few people realize or **appreciate** just how long popcorn has been **around**. Long **before** Columbus began his explorations, the **Indian** people of the Americas knew about popcorn. Unpopped kernels that are over a thousand years old have been discovered, still intact, in Peru. And popped corn more than five thousand years old has been found **buried** in a cave in New Mexico.

Checking Your Reading Power

Put an *x* in the box before the correct answer to each question.

Main Idea
1. This selection is mainly about
   - ☐ a. the Indian people of the Americas.
   - ☐ b. the history of corn.
   - ☐ c. how long popcorn has been around.

Supporting Details
2. Which of the following is true of popcorn kernels?
   - ☐ a. They are extremely soft.
   - ☐ b. They never explode.
   - ☐ c. They have waterproof shells.

Vocabulary in Context
3. What is the meaning of the word intact?
   - ☐ a. undamaged
   - ☐ b. broken
   - ☐ c. thoughtful

Cause and Effect
4. What causes popcorn to pop?
   - ☐ a. steam
   - ☐ b. cold water
   - ☐ c. air pressure

Inference
5. This passage suggests that popcorn
   - ☐ a. is purely an American treat.
   - ☐ b. was first grown in the Americas.
   - ☐ c. was eaten by Columbus on his voyage to America.

More Spelling Power to You

Look back over the boldfaced words in the passage. Pay close attention to how they are spelled. Then, in your notebook, write each word in a sentence and underline the spelling word.

At home, study the spellings of the underlined words. For some good spelling strategies, turn to page 8.

After you have studied the words, you will complete the spelling check on the next page. It contains some words from previous lessons, as well as most of the words from this lesson. So be sure to review all the words you have learned so far in this book. Concentrate especially on the list of words you misspelled on previous spelling checks.

Checking Your Spelling Power

Complete this exercise without looking back at the words. Each of the sentences below contains one misspelled word. Underline the misspelled word. Then write it correctly on the line to the left.

.... 1. If you try hard enough, you will eventuelly succeed.

.... 2. I apreciate winning, but on occasion one can learn a lesson by losing.

.... 3. Leon did not feel all right; he had a slight temperture and a stomachache.

.... 4. Leora is anxious to visit Acoma, where her favorite indian pottery is made.

.... 5. The frightened rabbit looked around, saw nothing, and hurried with releif straight toward its burrow.

.... 6. They planned an extremly large banquet to celebrate the happy occasion.

.... 7. It started as an ordinery day, but what happened later was truly amazing.

.... 8. A meteor, whose source was more than forty million miles away, fell to the earth and was buryed in the ground.

.... 9. Please arrive an hour befor the gates open, since attendance is expected to be high.

.... 10. When you feel strong enough to speak, describe exactly what did ocurr.

Check your answers in the answer key on page 100. In your notebook, keep a list of the words you misspelled. Study those words until you master them.

Words Often Confused and Misused

The words *your* and *you're* are commonly confused and misused. Like *its* and *it's,* as well as *whose* and *who's,* one word shows possession while the other is a contraction. Carefully study the meanings of the words and the sample sentences. Then do the exercise that follows.

your   The word *your* is a possessive pronoun meaning "belonging to you."

you're   The word *you're* is a contraction meaning "you are." The apostrophe takes the place of the letter *a* in *are.*

> Please introduce me to **your** brother and **your** sister, and say that I'm **your** favorite teacher.
> When **you're** right **you're** right, but when **you're** wrong **you're** wrong.
> **Your** report card shows that **you're** improving greatly.

Complete the sentences below by writing *your* and *you're* in the proper blanks.

1. Although .... the last person in line, ... turn will come before .... aware of it.

2. Perhaps you should make art .... career, since .... paintings demonstrate that .... very talented.

3. Now that .... doing so well, speak to .... employer about .... chances of getting a raise.

Now review the Words Often Confused and Misused from previous lessons. They will be included in the Cumulative Review following lesson 16.

UNIT 4
Presenting the Presidents

When you have completed this unit, you will have mastered 160 of the words that are most frequently misspelled and 33 words that are commonly confused and misused.

• 13 •

For seven years, President Theodore Roosevelt lived with a bullet in his chest. This strange story began in October 1912, when a man named John F. Schrank made an assassination **attempt** on the president. Schrank shot Roosevelt half an hour before the **chief** executive was about to make a **speech** in Milwaukee. The bullet, **fortunately**, struck a metal eyeglass case in Roosevelt's pocket and was diverted from his heart.

Roosevelt placed a **handkerchief** over the wound and ordered his aides to **proceed** to the auditorium. There he delivered his talk on **schedule**. Doctors later determined that it was **unnecessary** to remove the bullet. Roosevelt recovered **completely**, but for the last seven years of his life the bullet remained a **permanent** part of his body.

Checking Your Reading Power

Put an *x* in the box before the correct answer to each question.

Main Idea
1. This selection is mainly about
   - ☐ a. a speech that President Theodore Roosevelt made.
   - ☐ b. the result of an assassination attempt on President Theodore Roosevelt.
   - ☐ c. President Theodore Roosevelt's strength and determination.

Supporting Details
2. Theodore Roosevelt was shot
   - ☐ a. before making a speech in Milwaukee.
   - ☐ b. while making a speech in Milwaukee.
   - ☐ c. after making a speech in Milwaukee.

Vocabulary in Context
3. As used in this selection, diverted means
   - ☐ a. amused.
   - ☐ b. turned aside.
   - ☐ c. injured.

Cause and Effect
4. President Roosevelt's life was saved by
   - ☐ a. the quick work of his aides.
   - ☐ b. a team of doctors.
   - ☐ c. an eyeglass case in his pocket.

Inference
5. We may infer that President Roosevelt
   - ☐ a. eventually died from the bullet wound.
   - ☐ b. placed concern with his responsibilities over concern for his welfare.
   - ☐ c. later granted a pardon to John Schrank.

More Spelling Power to You

Look back over the boldfaced words in the passage. Pay close attention to how they are spelled. Then, in your notebook, write each word in a sentence and underline the spelling word.

At home, study the spellings of the underlined words. For some good spelling strategies, turn to page 8.

After you have studied the words, you will complete the spelling check on the next page. It contains some words from previous lessons, as well as most of the words from this lesson. So be sure to review all the words you have learned so far in this book. Concentrate especially on the list of words you misspelled on previous spelling checks.

Checking Your Spelling Power

Complete this exercise without looking back at the words. In each of the following groups of words, one of the words is misspelled. On the line to the left, write the letter of the misspelled word.

1. _____ a. soldier   b. cheif   c. ordinary
2. _____ a. speek   b. speech   c. cafeteria
3. _____ a. allways   b. attempt   c. approach
4. _____ a. hankerchief   b. prefer   c. guessed
5. _____ a. buried   b. permitted   c. unecessary
6. _____ a. disagreeable b. permenent   c. importance
7. _____ a. procede   b. conquer   c. although
8. _____ a. schedule   b. fourty   c. flies
9. _____ a. fortunatly   b. continually c. valuable
10. _____ a. salary   b. Indian   c. completly

Check your answers in the answer key on page 100. In your notebook, keep a list of the words you misspelled. Study those words until you master them.

Words Often Confused and Misused

The words *knew* and *new* are often confused and misused. Carefully study the meanings of the words and the sample sentences. Then do the exercise that follows.

knew The word *knew* is the past tense of the verb *know*.

new Something that is *new* is very recent or has never existed before.

Although he whistled cheerfully, Arnold **knew**, deep in his heart, that he was frightened.
According to an old saying, a **new** broom sweeps clean.
Every dawn a **new** day begins, Grace **knew**.

Complete the sentences below by writing *knew* and *new* in the proper blanks.

1. Nikki _____ that after he moved to a _____ neighborhood he would have to make _____ friends.

2. The _____ teacher said that she already _____ the name of every student in class.

3. When the football team failed to score in the first half, the coach _____ that it was time to try some _____ plays.

Now review the Words Often Confused and Misused from previous lessons. They will be included in the Cumulative Review following lesson 16.

• 14 •

Some historians **argue** that David Rice Atchinson was the **twelfth** president of the United States—for a day. Here is how they account for that unusual, if somewhat **humorous**, **occurrence**.

James K. Polk, the **eleventh** president, served his last day in office on Saturday, March 3, 1849. The new president, Zachary Taylor, **preferred** to celebrate his installation on Monday, March 5. It therefore appears that for one **calendar** day—Sunday, March 4—the office of the president was **vacant**.

The law at that time expressly stated that when there was **neither** a president nor a vice president in office, the president *pro tempore* of the Senate automatically became president. David Rice Atchinson was president *pro tempore* of the Senate on March 4. Therefore, some historians **consider** him the president of the United States for that day.

Checking Your Reading Power

Put an *x* in the box before the correct answer to each question.

Main Idea
1. This selection is mainly about
   ☐ a. how Zachary Taylor became president.
   ☐ b. why some people think David Rice Atchinson was president for a day.
   ☐ c. the president *pro tempore* of the Senate.

Supporting Details
2. President James K. Polk's last day in office was
   ☐ a. March 3, 1849.
   ☐ b. March 4, 1849.
   ☐ c. March 5, 1849.

Vocabulary in Context
3. In the passage, what is the meaning of the word expressly?
   ☐ a. plainly or clearly
   ☐ b. quickly or swiftly
   ☐ c. quietly or softly

Cause and Effect
4. By law, the president *pro tempore* of the Senate became president
   ☐ a. at the request of the president.
   ☐ b. when there was neither a president nor a vice president in office.
   ☐ c. as a result of a special election.

Inference
5. We may infer that
   ☐ a. most people think of David Rice Atchinson as the twelfth president.
   ☐ b. David Rice Atchinson signed several bills into law on the day he was president.
   ☐ c. David Rice Atchinson is not generally considered the twelfth president.

More Spelling Power to You

Look back over the boldfaced words in the passage. Pay close attention to how they are spelled. Then, in your notebook, write each word in a sentence and underline the spelling word.

At home, study the spellings of the underlined words. For some good spelling strategies, turn to page 8.

After you have studied the words, you will complete the spelling check on the next page. It contains some words from previous lessons, as well as most of the words from this lesson. So be sure to review all the words you have learned so far in this book. Concentrate especially on the list of words you misspelled on previous spelling checks.

Checking Your Spelling Power

Complete this exercise without looking back at the words. In each of the following pairs of words, one word is spelled incorrectly. Circle that word. Then write it correctly on the line to the left.

.... 1. favorite
                        vacent

.... 2. twelvth
                        busy

.... 3. argue
                        greatful

.... 4. temperature
                        concider

.... 5. prefered
                        accompany

.... 6. neither
                        surprize

.... 7. occurrance
                        attendance

.... 8. calender
                        occur

.... 9. eleventh
                        genuin

.... 10. humerous
                        balloon

Check your answers in the answer key on page 100. In your notebook, keep a list of the words you misspelled. Study those words until you master them.

Words Often Confused and Misused

The words *stationary* and *stationery* are commonly confused and misused. Carefully study the meanings of the words and the sample sentences. Then do the exercise that follows.

stationary   The word *stationary* means "not moving" or "not movable."

stationery   The word *stationery* means "writing paper" or "writing supplies."

    In some rooms in our school, the chairs are **stationary**.
    Lucille ordered two boxes of white **stationery**.
    If the bus remains **stationary** in this traffic jam, I will get to town too late to buy **stationery**.

Complete the sentences below by writing *stationary* and *stationery* in the proper blanks.

1. On top of the heavy, ... safe in the corner were several sheets of business ....

2. Ed found a letter written on purple .... under the .... bleachers in the gym.

3. Since the table was not .... , when it was bumped the milk spilled over onto the ....

Now review the Words Often Confused and Misused from previous lessons. They will be included in the Cumulative Review following lesson 16.

• 15 •

During his term in office, President Ulysses S. Grant was once arrested—for speeding.

The incident **occurred** when a police officer observed Grant racing along a Washington, D.C., street in his horse and buggy. After a long chase, the officer managed to **seize** the horse's bridle and bring the animal to a halt.

The discovery that the wrongdoer was the president served to **embarrass** the officer. He started to **apologize** and was reluctant to arrest the <u>dignitary</u>. Grant, however, acted in a completely **honorable** manner. He did not use the presidency as a **defense**, nor did he **hesitate** to assume **responsibility**. He insisted that the officer **pursue** the arrest. Because he did **exceed** the speed limit, Grant was later fined twenty dollars for the offense.

Checking Your Reading Power

Put an *x* in the box before the correct answer to each question.

Main Idea
1. This selection is mainly about
   - ☐ a. how a police officer became embarrassed.
   - ☐ b. how President Grant was once arrested for speeding.
   - ☐ c. the fine that President Grant received for speeding.

Supporting Details
2. After the officer spoke to Grant, the president
   - ☐ a. used the presidency as a defense.
   - ☐ b. refused to accept responsibility.
   - ☐ c. insisted that the officer make the arrest.

Vocabulary in Context
3. What is the meaning of the word <u>dignitary</u>?
   - ☐ a. person of high position
   - ☐ b. someone who is not well-known
   - ☐ c. gentle or kind

Cause and Effect
4. The officer was able to stop the horse and buggy by
   - ☐ a. blowing a whistle.
   - ☐ b. chasing the animal until it grew tired.
   - ☐ c. grabbing the horse's bridle.

Inference
5. We may infer that at the time Grant was president
   - ☐ a. police officers were more thoughtful than they are today.
   - ☐ b. presidents traveled with less protection than they do today.
   - ☐ c. there were many automobiles on the road.

More Spelling Power to You

Look back over the boldfaced words in the passage. Pay close attention to how they are spelled. Then, in your notebook, write each word in a sentence and underline the spelling word.

At home, study the spellings of the underlined words. For some good spelling strategies, turn to page 8.

After you have studied the words, you will complete the spelling check on the next page. It contains some words from previous lessons, as well as most of the words from this lesson. So be sure to review all the words you have learned so far in this book. Concentrate especially on the list of words you misspelled on previous spelling checks.

Checking Your Spelling Power

Complete this exercise without looking back at the words. In each of the following groups of words, one word is misspelled. Circle the misspelled word. Then write it correctly on the line to the left.

....	1. hezitate	million	often	across
....	2. weigh	sieze	probably	around
....	3. anxious	apologize	prefer	argu
....	4. appreciate	exhibit	honerable	occasion
....	5. persue	extremely	banquet	restaurant
....	6. embarass	having	library	all right
....	7. speech	responsability	courageous	forward
....	8. generally	until	twelfth	defence
....	9. written	fortunately	occured	therefore
....	10. excede	unnecessary	handkerchief	business

Check your answers in the answer key on page 100. In your notebook, keep a list of the words you misspelled. Study those words until you master them.

Words Often Confused and Misused

The words *all together* and *altogether* are frequently confused and misused. Carefully study the meanings of the words and the sample sentences. Then do the exercise that follows.

all together   The words *all together* mean "everybody or everything together in the same place."

altogether   The word *altogether* means "entirely."

As soon as the group was **all together**, Bob snapped the picture.
His idea of how it should be done is **altogether** different from my own.
If we work **all together**, it's **altogether** possible that we'll finish on time.

Complete the sentences below by writing *all together* and *altogether* in the proper blanks.

1. I think Thanksgiving is .... delightful, because that's the time when my family is ....

2. The conductor called us .... to say that the music was .... too difficult to learn by next week.

3. Although the farm was .... destroyed by the fire, the farmer got his horses .... and rushed them to safety.

Now review the Words Often Confused and Misused from previous lessons. They will be included in the Cumulative Review following lesson 16.

•16•

Who was the best president and who was the worst? It's all a matter of personal **opinion**. But consider the following questions about the presidents. The answers rely upon facts rather than upon **judgment**.

Who was the shortest president of the United States? Without **doubt**, it was James Madison, the **fourth** president. He stood five feet four inches tall.

Who was the tallest president? If you **answered** "Abraham Lincoln," that was **excellent**. Lincoln was six feet four inches in height. Lyndon Baines Johnson, at six feet three inches, was nearly as tall.

Can you identify the largest president? It was **certainly** William Howard Taft, a man of remarkably imposing **appearance**. Taft stood six feet tall and weighed **approximately** 350 pounds. It is said that he had a special bathtub built in the White House to **accommodate** his great girth.

Checking Your Reading Power

Put an *x* in the box before the correct answer to each question.

Main Idea
1. This selection is mainly about
   - ☐ a. Abraham Lincoln and Lyndon B. Johnson.
   - ☐ b. the shortest president of the United States.
   - ☐ c. the sizes of the presidents.

Supporting Details
2. How tall was James Madison?
   - ☐ a. five feet four inches
   - ☐ b. six feet
   - ☐ c. six feet four inches

Vocabulary in Context
3. What is the meaning of the word girth?
   - ☐ a. height
   - ☐ b. weight
   - ☐ c. measurement around a body

Cause and Effect
4. Taft had a special bathtub built because
   - ☐ a. he was so large.
   - ☐ b. he was so short.
   - ☐ c. the old bathtub was broken.

Inference
5. This passage suggests that
   - ☐ a. one must be at least six feet tall to become president.
   - ☐ b. most presidents were short.
   - ☐ c. presidents have come in all sizes.

More Spelling Power to You

Look back over the boldfaced words in the passage. Pay close attention to how they are spelled. Then, in your notebook, write each word in a sentence and underline the spelling word.

At home, study the spellings of the underlined words. For some good spelling strategies, turn to page 8.

After you have studied the words, you will complete the spelling check on the next page. It contains some words from previous lessons, as well as most of the words from this lesson. So be sure to review all the words you have learned so far in this book. Concentrate especially on the list of words you misspelled on previous spelling checks.

Checking Your Spelling Power

Complete this exercise without looking back at the words. Each of the sentences below contains one misspelled word. Underline the misspelled word. Then write it correctly on the line before the sentence.

1. Babe Ruth finished an absolutely glorious career by hitting a home run in his last appearence at bat.

2. Consuelo ansered the questions by using the books she found in the library.

3. Everyone held a different opinion about how the terrible accident had ocurred.

4. *The Red Badge of Courage,* written in 1895, certanly offers a brilliant description of a person's feelings during war.

5. There is no dout that Bill's explanation makes sense.

6. John James Audubon, an excellent artist, usally preferred to draw pictures of the birds he'd been studying.

7. I must apologize for making an error in judgment.

8. The clerk said, "I believe we will be able to acommodate you if we receive your request this week."

9. If people keep coming to our games, attendance should far exceed that of last season and reach approximitely two thousand.

10. Her fourth attempt was a bit awkward; therefor Ann did not get a perfect score in diving.

Check your answers in the answer key on page 100. In your notebook, keep a list of the words you misspelled. Study those words until you master them.

Words Often Confused and Misused

The words *brake* and *break* are frequently confused and misused. Carefully study the meanings of the words and the sample sentences. Then do the exercise that follows.

brake   The word *brake* refers to "anything that slows or stops a moving vehicle."

break   The word *break* means "to shatter or smash."

Every car needs a good emergency **brake.**
A bull in a china shop is bound to **break** something.
If you ride a bicycle without a **brake**, you might **break** some bones.

Complete the sentences below by writing *brake* and *break* in the proper blanks.

1. The _____ on one of my roller skates happened to _____ .

2. Don't _____ the law; be sure that the _____ on your car is working.

3. When the _____ on her bicycle failed to operate, Rita was lucky she didn't _____ her arm.

Now review the Words Often Confused and Misused from lessons 1–16. They will be included in the Cumulative Review that begins on the next page.

Cumulative Review of Units 1-4

I. In each of the following groups of words, one word is misspelled. Circle the misspelled word. Then write the word correctly on the line to the left.

1. completely
   exceede
   hesitate

2. embarras
   surprise
   sense

3. suppose
   beginning
   quantaty

4. importance
   praferred
   forty

5. occurrence
   balloon
   humerus

6. Indian
   critacism
   recognize

7. relief
   opinon
   terrible

8. across
   dapendent
   interrupt

9. judgement
   library
   toward

10. occasion
    biggest
    accomodate

II. Fill in the blanks in the words to create words that are spelled correctly. Then write the words on the lines to the left.

1. d_scribe
2. con_ider
3. appear_nce
4. exist_nce
5. exc_ll_nt
6. ap_l_gize
7. caf_t_ria
8. approx_m_tely
9. perm_n_nt
10. r_spons_b_l_ty

III. The letters *ie* or *ei* are missing from each of the words below. Fill in the blanks in each word to spell the word correctly. Then write the word on the line to the left.

1. ch_ _f
2. n_ _ther
3. s_ _ze
4. bel_ _ve
5. w_ _gh

IV. In each of the following sentences, one of the four underlined words is misspelled. Circle the misspelled word. Then write the word correctly on the line before the sentence.

1. In an absolutely brilliant speech, Mark Antony said that Caesar's murderers were all honerable men.

2. Please check your skedule to see if you can meet me on the fourth, the eleventh, or the twelfth.

3. Myrna eventually was able to conquer her fear of high places; now she often flys without concern.

4. Almost nothing is impossible if you continually try untill you succeed.

5. Without doubt, Ted's attendance is truely extraordinary.

6. When the temprature is extremely high, people always ask, "Is it hot enough for you?"

7. You will discover that it is certainly better to give than to recieve—especially if you are having a fight.

8. The office is usually busy, but if you arrive early you will probably be able to speek to Mr. James.

9. When the tightrope walker accidentally slipped, there was great excitement; fortunately, she was alright.

10. The novel is still interesting and fascinating, althogh it was written many years ago.

V. Each of the following sentences contains two words in parentheses. Underline the one that makes the sentence correct. Then write the word on the line to the left.

1. Once, many years ago, our old car was (knew, new).

2. A sign in large letters said, "Watch (your, you're) hat and coat."

3. When we went on vacation, it rained all (weak, week).

4. The Pacific Ocean is larger (than, then) the Atlantic Ocean.

5. What time is it in Paris when (its, it's) ten o'clock in New York?

6. The waiter said, "Don't mention that there's a fly in your soup or everyone else will want one (to, too, two)."

7. In the morning, I can't decide (weather, whether) to get out of bed on the left side or the right side.

8. The conductor asked the students in the orchestra, "Are you (all ready, already) to play?"

9. If you want to write a letter on black (stationary, stationery), you must use white ink.

10. On stage Joel is showy and loud; offstage he is soft-spoken and (quiet, quite).

11. Please (accept, except) our thanks for a job well done.

12. It is likely that their concert will (brake, break) all records.

13. Are you the girl (whose, who's) dog ate my book?

14. I thought I might (loose, lose) the race when I saw that I was last.

15. The Mississippi River flows (threw, through) ten states.

UNIT 5
Literary Folk

When you have completed this unit, you will have mastered 200 of the words that are most frequently misspelled and 41 words that are commonly confused and misused.

• 17 •

You **remember** Alice, of course. She is the girl who **dropped** into a hole while **running** after a white rabbit that was **hurrying** along. What followed were the adventures of Alice in Wonderland.

Before Alice returned home from Wonderland, she made the **acquaintance** of many **weird** and wonderful creatures. Among them were the Mad Hatter, the Mock Turtle, and the Queen of Hearts.

Alice's creator, Lewis Carroll, was a **professor** of mathematics at a **college** in England. Carroll wrote *Alice in Wonderland* **especially** for a little girl named Alice Liddell, the daughter of a friend. He made up the story of Alice one day in 1862, while they were **picnicking**. Over time he began to embellish, or add details to, the story. Three years later, *Alice's Adventures in Wonderland* was published. It has long been a favorite children's book.

Checking Your Reading Power

Put an *x* in the box before the correct answer to each question.

Main Idea
1. This selection is mainly about
   - ☐ a. Alice Liddell.
   - ☐ b. the Mad Hatter.
   - ☐ c. *Alice in Wonderland* and its author.

Supporting Details
2. Lewis Carroll wrote *Alice in Wonderland*
   - ☐ a. for some students at a college.
   - ☐ b. for the daughter of a friend.
   - ☐ c. because he needed money.

Vocabulary in Context
3. As used in this selection, what does the word embellish mean?
   - ☐ a. to go on a picnic
   - ☐ b. to go to a strange land
   - ☐ c. to add details to a story

Cause and Effect
4. Alice's adventures in Wonderland began when she
   - ☐ a. dropped into a hole while chasing a rabbit.
   - ☐ b. met the Queen of Hearts.
   - ☐ c. went to a college in England.

Inference
5. We may infer that *Alice in Wonderland* was first published in
   - ☐ a. 1862.
   - ☐ b. 1865.
   - ☐ c. 1859.

More Spelling Power to You

Look back over the boldfaced words in the passage. Pay close attention to how they are spelled. Then, in your notebook, write each word in a sentence and underline the spelling word.

At home, study the spellings of the underlined words. For some good spelling strategies, turn to page 8.

After you have studied the words, you will complete the spelling check on the next page. It contains some words from previous lessons, as well as most of the words from this lesson. So be sure to review all the words you have learned so far in this book. Concentrate especially on the list of words you misspelled on previous spelling checks.

Checking Your Spelling Power

Complete this exercise without looking back at the words. In each of the following groups of words, one of the words is misspelled. On the line to the left, write the letter of the misspelled word.

1. .... a. occur   b. proffessor   c. across
2. .... a. dropped   b. permited   c. genuine
3. .... a. appreciate   b. happened   c. colledge
4. .... a. wierd   b. soldier   c. before
5. .... a. especialy   b. buried   c. prefer
6. .... a. akwaintance   b. ordinary   c. defense
7. .... a. embarrass   b. consider   c. picknicking
8. .... a. remember   b. favrite   c. conquer
9. .... a. around   b. runing   c. written
10. .... a. hurryng   b. valuable   c. similar

Check your answers in the answer key on page 101. In your notebook, keep a list of the words you misspelled. Study those words until you master them.

Words Often Confused and Misused

Because they sound alike, the words *hear* and *here* are often confused and misused. Carefully study the meanings of the words and the sample sentences. Then do the exercise that follows.

hear The word *hear* means "to take in sounds through the ear."

here The word *here* means "in this place."

When did you **hear** the good news?
Let's all meet **here** on Thursday.
Speak into the microphone so that everyone **here** will be able to **hear** you.

Complete the sentences below by writing *hear* and *here* in the proper blanks.

1. As soon as you .... the starter's gun, race from .... to the finish line.
2. Perhaps we should camp ...., for I .... that rain is on the way.
3. I was sorry to .... of his illness, but I realized that something was the matter when I did not see him ....

Now review the Words Often Confused and Misused from previous lessons. They will be included in the Cumulative Review that follows lesson 24.

• 18 •

Washington Irving was the first American **author** to earn a living by **writing**. Famous in his day, today Irving is probably best known as the creator of the fictional character Rip Van Winkle.

Rip is one of Irving's most popular **heroes**. In the story entitled "Rip Van Winkle," Rip takes a nap that lasts for twenty years. When he falls asleep in 1756, the thirteen American colonies are under the <u>domination</u> of King George of England. When he awakes two decades later, the colonies have become a **democracy**, **independent** of England.

Rip, of course, was in a **vacuum** while that great change was taking place, and he awakes **ignorant** of what happened during his **absence**. He doesn't **realize** that while he was sleeping he became a citizen of the new United States of America. He is so confused by the changes he finds around him that he feels like a visitor in a **foreign** land.

Checking Your Reading Power

Put an *x* in the box before the correct answer to each question.

Main Idea

1. This selection is mainly about
   - ☐ a. England's colonization of North America.
   - ☐ b. Rip Van Winkle.
   - ☐ c. how the colonies became independent of England.

Supporting Details

2. Washington Irving was the first American author to
   - ☐ a. earn a living by writing.
   - ☐ b. become a citizen of the United States.
   - ☐ c. fight for the colonies.

Vocabulary in Context

3. What is the meaning of the word <u>domination</u>?
   - ☐ a. cruelty
   - ☐ b. flag
   - ☐ c. rule

Cause and Effect

4. Today, Irving's reputation is based mainly on
   - ☐ a. one story he wrote.
   - ☐ b. his novels of adventure.
   - ☐ c. his support of democracy.

Inference

5. If someone calls you a Rip Van Winkle, that person is probably suggesting that you
   - ☐ a. enjoy working very hard.
   - ☐ b. are very bright.
   - ☐ c. are out of touch with what's happening around you.

More Spelling Power to You

Look back over the boldfaced words in the passage. Pay close attention to how they are spelled. Then, in your notebook, write each word in a sentence and underline the spelling word.

At home, study the spellings of the underlined words. For some good spelling strategies, turn to page 8.

After you have studied the words, you will complete the spelling check on the next page. It contains some words from previous lessons, as well as most of the words from this lesson. So be sure to review all the words you have learned so far in this book. Concentrate especially on the list of words you misspelled on previous spelling checks.

Checking Your Spelling Power

Complete this exercise without looking back at the words. In each of the following pairs of words, one word is spelled incorrectly. Circle that word. Then write it correctly on the line to the left.

.... 1. writting
                       professor

.... 2. salary
                       independant

.... 3. payed
                       realize

.... 4. author
                       remembar

.... 5. heros
                       library

.... 6. suppose
                       democrasy

.... 7. vacum
                       straight

.... 8. ignorant
                       especialy

.... 9. existance
                       foreign

.... 10. absense
                       impossible

Check your answers in the answer key on page 101. In your notebook, keep a list of the words you misspelled. Study those words until you master them.

Words Often Confused and Misused

The words *shone* and *shown* are frequently confused and misused. Carefully study the meanings of the words and the sample sentences. Then do the exercise that follows.

shone   The word *shone* is the past tense of *shine*.

shown   The word *shown* is the past participle of *show,* meaning "to reveal or make known."

From the first day of our vacation, the sun has not **shone**.
How many times has he **shown** you his stamp collection?
When she had **shown** us how the trick was done, the magician's eyes **shone** with delight.

Complete the sentences below by writing *shone* and *shown* in the proper blanks.

1. The moon .... down on the pyramids that our guide had just .... us.

2. When her project was .... to the class, Marilyn's eyes .... with delight.

3. Because the light .... into the room, the movie was not ....

Now review the Words Often Confused and Misused from previous lessons. They will be included in the Cumulative Review following lesson 24.

• 19 •

The novel *Don Quixote* is one of the masterpieces of world **literature**. Written by Miguel de Cervantes, its main **character** is the wonderful Don Quixote.

Cervantes' story <u>recounts</u> the tale of a middle-aged landowner who sees himself as a knight of old. It tells how he dresses in armor and **announces** that he is Don Quixote of La Mancha. He sets out, **committed** to battle for justice, with his faithful companion, Sancho Panza.

A man of great **conscience**, Don Quixote attempts to **achieve** victory over evil. He is fearless, **stubborn**, courageous, and proud. Sometimes he is also silly. Sancho Panza, on the other hand, is always **sensible** and cautious. The two have many **amusing** adventures **together**. In one famous episode, Don Quixote attacks a group of windmills, which he thinks are giants.

○ Checking Your Reading Power ○

Put an *x* in the box before the correct answer to each question.

Main Idea
1. This selection is mainly about
   - ☐ a. Sancho Panza.
   - ☐ b. Don Quixote.
   - ☐ c. Miguel de Cervantes.

Supporting Details
2. Don Quixote was a
   - ☐ a. knight of old.
   - ☐ b. Spanish landowner.
   - ☐ c. famous writer.

Vocabulary in Context
3. What is the meaning of the word <u>recounts</u>?
   - ☐ a. counts again
   - ☐ b. hears
   - ☐ c. tells

Cause and Effect
4. Don Quixote attacked some windmills because he
   - ☐ a. thought they were giants.
   - ☐ b. thought his enemies were hiding inside them.
   - ☐ c. hated windmills.

Inference
5. We may infer that Don Quixote
   - ☐ a. was a coward.
   - ☐ b. had a lively imagination.
   - ☐ c. always listened to Sancho Panza.

○ More Spelling Power to You ○

Look back over the boldfaced words in the passage. Pay close attention to how they are spelled. Then, in your notebook, write each word in a sentence and underline the spelling word.

At home, study the spellings of the underlined words. For some good spelling strategies, turn to page 8.

After you have studied the words, you will complete the spelling check on the next page. It contains some words from previous lessons, as well as most of the words from this lesson. So be sure to review all the words you have learned so far in this book. Concentrate especially on the list of words you misspelled on previous spelling checks.

Checking Your Spelling Power

Complete this exercise without looking back at the words. In each of the following groups of words, one word is misspelled. Circle the misspelled word. Then write it correctly on the line to the left.

....	1. amuseing	writing	losing	making
....	2. acquaintance	twelfth	until	litrature
....	3. stubborn	auther	usually	forty
....	4. college	source	anounces	familiar
....	5. concience	picnicking	vacuum	honorable
....	6. height	achieve	sandwich	facinating
....	7. heroes	ignorent	weird	together
....	8. sensable	independent	pursue	running
....	9. hurrying	democracy	commited	equipped
....	10. calendar	charactor	absence	necessary

Check your answers in the answer key on page 101. In your notebook, keep a list of the words you misspelled. Study those words until you master them.

Words Often Confused and Misused

The words *peace* and *piece* are commonly confused and misused. Carefully study the meanings of the words and the sample sentences. Then do the exercise that follows.

peace The word *peace* means "calmness and stillness" or "absence of war."

piece The word *piece* means "a part of something."

The two countries had always lived together in **peace**.
May I have a very small **piece** of cake?
Since he received that **piece** of bad news, he has known no **peace**.

Complete the sentences below by writing *peace* and *piece* in the proper blanks.

1. The .... treaty was written on a .... of white paper.

2. Audrey munched on a .... of apple, and happily enjoyed the .... and quiet of the country.

3. A dispute over a tiny .... of land suddenly broke the ....

Now review the Words Often Confused and Misused from previous lessons. They will be included in the Cumulative Review following lesson 24.

• 20 •

An **ancient** Greek myth tells the sad story of Orpheus and Eurydice. Orpheus was a poet and musician. So sweetly did he play the lyre that he could charm wild beasts and even trees and rocks.

Orpheus fell in love with the beautiful Eurydice and married her. But soon after the **marriage**, death came like a **thief** and took Eurydice. How Orpheus did **grieve**! Filled with **despair**, he decided to **descend** to the land of the dead to try to get her back. There he met Pluto, who ruled that dark <u>domain</u>.

Orpheus begged for Eurydice's return. He played his lyre for Pluto. So **beautiful** was his song and so **sincerely** did he plead that he was able to **persuade** Pluto to make a bargain. "Eurydice may follow behind you to the land of the living," said Pluto. "But if you look back at her before you arrive, she will **disappear**."

Joyfully, Orpheus led Eurydice to the land of the living. As he stepped into the sunlight, he turned to welcome her into his arms. But Eurydice was still in the gloom. As soon as Orpheus glimpsed her shadowy form, she disappeared into the darkness, uttering only a faint "Farewell."

Checking Your Reading Power

Put an *x* in the box before the correct answer to each question.

Main Idea
1. This selection is mainly about
   - ☐ a. the story of Orpheus and Eurydice.
   - ☐ b. the ancient Greeks.
   - ☐ c. ancient Greek myths.

Supporting Details
2. Orpheus was a wonderful
   - ☐ a. writer.
   - ☐ b. magician.
   - ☐ c. musician.

Vocabulary in Context
3. What is the meaning of the word <u>domain</u>?
   - ☐ a. land
   - ☐ b. sleep
   - ☐ c. rock

Cause and Effect
4. Orpheus lost Eurydice forever because
   - ☐ a. she no longer loved him.
   - ☐ b. Pluto refused to let her return to the land of the living.
   - ☐ c. he looked back at her.

Inference
5. After Eurydice disappeared, Orpheus probably
   - ☐ a. went back to talk to Pluto again.
   - ☐ b. was overcome with sorrow.
   - ☐ c. believed that Eurydice would return one day.

More Spelling Power to You

Look back over the boldfaced words in the passage. Pay close attention to how they are spelled. Then, in your notebook, write each word in a sentence and underline the spelling word.

At home, study the spellings of the underlined words. For some spelling strategies, turn to page 8.

After you have studied the words, you will complete the spelling check on the next page. It contains some words from previous lessons, as well as most of the words from this lesson. So be sure to review all the words you have learned so far in this book. Concentrate especially on the list of words you have misspelled on previous spelling checks.

Checking Your Spelling Power

Complete this exercise without looking back at the words. Each of the sentences below contains one misspelled word. Underline the misspelled word. Then write it correctly on the line before the sentence.

.... 1. The victim of the crime was able to recognize the theif at once.

.... 2. On Sunday, they will celebrate the fourth anniversary of their marrage.

.... 3. After his team committed its sixth error, the coach was filled with a sense of dispair.

.... 4. On the walls of the cave you will discover ancient paintings that are very intresting.

.... 5. Please accept my apology; I am sincerly sorry for the confusion that occurred.

.... 6. Moments after the banquet ended, the guests headed toward the exit and began to disapear.

.... 7. This is probably the most beautyful work of literature I have ever read.

.... 8. In case of fire, remember to decend the stairs and proceed directly to the street.

.... 9. It is certainly not unusual for a child to greive over the loss of a pet.

.... 10. As a leader, she was known for excellent judgement and for the ability to persuade her followers.

Check your answers in the answer key on page 101. In your notebook, keep a list of the words you misspelled. Study those words until you master them.

Words Often Confused and Misused

The words *advice* and *advise* are often confused and misused. Carefully study the meanings of the words and the sample sentences. Then do the exercise that follows.

advice   The noun *advice* (ad-VICE) means "an opinion or suggestion about what should be done."

advise   The verb *advise* (ad-VIZE) means "to give an opinion or advice."

Thank you for your excellent **advice**.
If you wish to be a better tennis player, I **advise** you to practice more.
The judge said, "I **advise** you to follow my **advice**."

Complete the sentences below by writing *advice* and *advise* in the proper blanks.

1. I'd .... you to speak to a travel agent for .... about London.

2. "We can .... you," said the coach, "but you must decide whether or not to follow our ...."

3. Few things are as valuable and inexpensive as good .... ; I .... you to remember that.

Now review the Words Often Confused and Misused from previous lessons. They will be included in the Cumulative Review that follows lesson 24.

64

UNIT 6
Strange Stuff

When you have completed this unit, you will have mastered 240 of the words that are most frequently misspelled and 49 words that are commonly confused and misused.

• 21 •

Draw an **imaginary** line from Florida to Puerto Rico to Bermuda and back to Florida. That area of the Atlantic is known as the Bermuda Triangle. For more than a hundred years, ships and planes have seemingly vanished within the **boundary** of the triangle.

On December 5, 1945, for example, five U.S. Navy planes left Fort Lauderdale, Florida, on a training mission. An hour later, all the planes began to **experience** problems. Their compasses were suddenly incapable of giving an **accurate** reading. The **lieutenant** in charge of the mission radioed the control tower: "Everything is wrong. We are completely lost."

A rescue plane **carrying** emergency **equipment** was dispatched at once. Neither it nor the other five planes were seen or heard from **again**.

There is no completely **satisfactory** explanation for the **tragedy**. But this much can be said: all the planes were lost in the Bermuda Triangle.

Checking Your Reading Power

Put an *x* in the box before the correct answer to each question.

Main Idea
1. This selection is mainly about
   - ☐ a. why ships and planes have been lost near Bermuda.
   - ☐ b. a famous air rescue.
   - ☐ c. an event that took place in the Bermuda Triangle.

Supporting Details
2. The Bermuda Triangle is
   - ☐ a. an imaginary line over Florida.
   - ☐ b. an area in the Atlantic Ocean.
   - ☐ c. the area between Puerto Rico and Bermuda.

Vocabulary in Context
3. What is the meaning of the word incapable?
   - ☐ a. able
   - ☐ b. unable
   - ☐ c. false

Cause and Effect
4. What caused the tragedy in the Bermuda Triangle?
   - ☐ a. A sudden storm arose.
   - ☐ b. The planes ran out of gas.
   - ☐ c. There is no completely satisfactory explanation.

Inference
5. This selection suggests that
   - ☐ a. strange forces may be at work in the Bermuda Triangle.
   - ☐ b. compasses often give readings that are not accurate.
   - ☐ c. the Navy pilots were not following orders.

More Spelling Power to You

Look back over the boldfaced words in the passage. Pay close attention to how they are spelled. Then, in your notebook, write each word in a sentence and underline the spelling word.

At home, study the spellings of the underlined words. For some good spelling strategies, turn to page 8.

After you have studied the words, you will complete the spelling check on the next page. It contains some words from previous lessons, as well as most of the words from this lesson. So be sure to review all the words you have learned so far in this book. Concentrate especially on the list of words you misspelled on previous spelling checks.

Checking Your Spelling Power

Complete this exercise without looking back at the words. In each of the following groups of words, one of the words is misspelled. On the line to the left, write the letter of the misspelled word.

1. _____ a. again   b. ammong   c. amusing
2. _____ a. boundry   b. career   c. disappear
3. _____ a. ache   b. sincerely   c. experiance
4. _____ a. leutenant   b. foreign   c. descend
5. _____ a. announce   b. satisfactary c. exhibit
6. _____ a. beautiful   b. acurate   c. conscience
7. _____ a. character   b. imaginery   c. nonsense
8. _____ a. realise   b. heroes   c. tragedy
9. _____ a. guessed   b. marriage   c. equiptment
10. _____ a. carrying   b. stuborn   c. despair

Check your answers in the answer key on page 101. In your notebook, keep a list of the words you misspelled. Study those words until you master them.

Words Often Confused and Misused

The words *principal* and *principle* are commonly confused and misused. Carefully study the meanings of the words and the sample sentences. Then do the exercise that follows.

principal The word *principal* means "most important or main." It may also mean "the leader or head of a school."

principle The word *principle* means "a basic rule, truth, or law."

Our **principal** was the **principal** speaker.
She believes in the **principle** that honesty is the best policy.
The **principal** parts of the verb were listed in the chapter on the **principles** of grammar.

Complete the sentences below by writing *principal* and *principle* in the proper blanks.

1. Mr. Harvey, the _____ , showed the new students the _____ parts of the school.
2. The _____ of free speech was the _____ subject of the talk.
3. The _____ asked us to state one _____ that we believe in.

Now review the Words Often Confused and Misused from previous lessons. They will be included in the Cumulative Review that follows lesson 24.

•22•

The "**eighth** wonder of the world" was discovered in 1869 on a farm in Cardiff, New York. Workers digging a well there uncovered a large stone figure buried in the ground. It was ten feet long and weighed three thousand pounds. While opinion about the find was **divided**, some "scientists" said that it was the petrified remains of an ancient giant man.

When people **heard** the news, they **immediately** rushed to the **scene**. They paid fifty cents each for the **privilege** of seeing the giant.

Two months later, some facts about the Cardiff Giant came to light. The figure had been carved from stone by stonecutters in Chicago. The huge statue had then been **transferred** to the farm, where it was buried in the earth. It was all part of a get-rich-quick **scheme planned** by an **individual** named George Hull. The "eighth wonder of the world" had been a giant <u>hoax</u>.

Checking Your Reading Power

Put an *x* in the box before the correct answer to each question.

Main Idea
1. This selection is mainly about
   - ☐ a. the Cardiff Giant.
   - ☐ b. George Hull.
   - ☐ c. the greatest hoaxes of all time.

Supporting Details
2. The Cardiff Giant was
   - ☐ a. the remains of an early giant man.
   - ☐ b. ten feet long.
   - ☐ c. carved from stone in New York.

Vocabulary in Context
3. What is the meaning of the word <u>hoax</u>?
   - ☐ a. trick
   - ☐ b. carver
   - ☐ c. robbery

Cause and Effect
4. People rushed to Cardiff, New York, to
   - ☐ a. look for other stone giants.
   - ☐ b. meet with some scientists.
   - ☐ c. see a stone giant.

Inference
5. The quotation marks around the word *scientists* suggest that
   - ☐ a. the people weren't really scientists.
   - ☐ b. the scientists were very well-known.
   - ☐ c. scientists are never wrong.

More Spelling Power to You

Look back over the boldfaced words in the passage. Pay close attention to how they are spelled. Then, in your notebook, write each word in a sentence and underline the spelling word.

At home, study the spellings of the underlined words. For some good spelling strategies, turn to page 8.

After you have studied the words, you will complete the spelling check on the next page. It contains some words from previous lessons, as well as most of the words from this lesson. So be sure to review all the words you have learned so far in this book. Concentrate especially on the list of words you misspelled on previous spelling checks.

Checking Your Spelling Power

Complete this exercise without looking back at the words. In each of the following pairs of words, one word is spelled incorrectly. Circle that word. Then write it correctly on the line to the left.

1. heard
   anceint

2. devided
   imaginary

3. imediately
   experience

4. trully
   planned

5. skeme
   lieutenant

6. boundary
   priviledge

7. eigth
   attendance

8. scene
   tradgedy

9. transfered
   equipment

10. grievous
    individuel

Check your answers in the answer key on page 101. In your notebook, keep a list of the words you misspelled. Study those words until you master them.

Words Often Confused and Misused

The words *past* and *passed* are frequently confused and misused. Carefully study the meanings of the words and the sample sentences. Then do the exercise that follows.

past The word *past* means "just finished or ended." It sometimes refers to "a time gone by."

passed The word *passed* is the past tense of the verb "to pass," which means "to go by."

For the **past** month, the weather has been beautiful.
Putting on a burst of speed, Sue **passed** the other runners.
Adele **passed** all the subjects she took this **past** year.

Complete the sentences below by writing *past* and *passed* in the proper blanks.

1. Jason _____ the hours reading about great scientists of the _____ .

2. In a _____ game, the quarterback _____ for more than three hundred yards.

3. Now that the final exam was _____ , Gloria was anxious to know if she had _____ chemistry.

Now review the Words Often Confused and Misused from previous lessons. They will be included in the Cumulative Review that follows lesson 24.

•23•

On a **pleasant** day in 1872, the British ship *Dei Gratia* was on its way to Spain. When the *Dei Gratia* was **almost** six hundred miles off the coast of Gibraltar, the lookout became **conscious** of a ship in the distance. It seemed to just be drifting <u>randomly</u> on the quiet sea.

The *Dei Gratia*'s **captain** thought that perhaps the ship needed **assistance**. So he ordered some of his men to board it at once. They discovered that the name of the ship was the *Mary Celeste*. It was **evidently** in excellent condition—clean, dry, and well stocked with food. Its cargo was untouched. There were no **noticeable** signs of struggle or flight. Everything seemed normal—*but there was no one on board!*

The men searched the ship **thoroughly**. They were looking for a clue to what had happened to the crew. But nothing they found would **yield** an answer. To this day, no one **really** knows what happened to the passengers and crew of the *Mary Celeste*.

Checking Your Reading Power

Put an *x* in the box before the correct answer to each question.

Main Idea
1. This selection is mainly about
   - ☐ a. the mystery of the *Mary Celeste*.
   - ☐ b. the captain of the British ship *Dei Gratia*.
   - ☐ c. the dangers of sailing ships.

Supporting Details
2. Which one of the following was true of the *Mary Celeste*?
   - ☐ a. There were signs of a struggle on the boat.
   - ☐ b. The ship was in poor condition.
   - ☐ c. The boat was well stocked with food.

Vocabulary in Context
3. What is the meaning of the word <u>randomly</u>?
   - ☐ a. silently
   - ☐ b. aimlessly
   - ☐ c. quickly

Cause and Effect
4. The captain ordered some men to board the *Mary Celeste* because he
   - ☐ a. knew that there was no one on the ship.
   - ☐ b. thought that the ship needed help.
   - ☐ c. was following orders to search the boat.

Inference
5. We may infer that the passengers and crew of the *Mary Celeste* had not been lost in a storm, because the
   - ☐ a. boat was found on a pleasant day.
   - ☐ b. ship's cargo was untouched.
   - ☐ c. boat was dry and in good condition.

More Spelling Power to You

Look back over the boldfaced words in the passage. Pay close attention to how they are spelled. Then, in your notebook, write each word in a sentence and underline the spelling word.

At home, study the spellings of the underlined words. For some good spelling strategies, turn to page 8.

After you have studied the words, you will complete the spelling check on the next page. It contains some words from previous lessons, as well as most of the words from this lesson. So be sure to review all the words you have learned so far in this book. Concentrate especially on the list of words you misspelled on previous spelling checks.

Checking Your Spelling Power

Complete this exercise without looking back at the words. In each of the following groups of words, one word is misspelled. Circle the misspelled word. Then write it correctly on the line to the left.

....	1. immediately	realy	transferred	terrible
....	2. allmost	all right	although	always
....	3. college	privilege	captin	accurate
....	4. scene	scheme	concious	absence
....	5. eighth	throughly	extraordinary	vacuum
....	6. asistence	especially	stubborn	accompany
....	7. yield	acheive	busy	divided
....	8. literature	enough	carryng	evidently
....	9. pleasent	appearance	individual	doubt
....	10. using	equipment	noticable	tragedy

Check your answers in the answer key on page 101. In your notebook, keep a list of the words you misspelled. Study those words until you master them.

Words Often Confused and Misused

The words *miner* and *minor* are sometimes confused and misused. Carefully study the meanings of the words and the sample sentences. Then do the exercise that follows.

miner The word *miner* means "a person who works in a mine."

minor The word *minor* means "less important or smaller." It may also mean "a person who is not yet of legal age."

The work of a **miner** is often very difficult.
The lawyer raised a **minor** objection because the key witness was still a **minor**.
He could not be employed as a **miner** until he was no longer a **minor**.

Complete the sentences below by writing *miner* and *minor* in the proper blanks.

1. Julio's paper about the life of a coal .... contained only a few .... typing errors.

2. Although she was still a .... and could not yet vote, Leah did not consider voting a .... responsibility.

3. As a young man, George worked as a .... in the hills of West Virginia, but years later he gained a bit of fame as a .... poet.

Now review the Words Often Confused and Misused from previous lessons. They will be included in the Cumulative Review that follows lesson 24.

•24•

In remote parts of China, villagers have sometimes told of seeing a hairy, two-legged beast more than seven feet tall. The creature is **referred** to as the wild man, or Ye Ren.

According to reports, Ye Ren walks upright, has thick hair all over its body, and does not **possess** a tail. It is not afraid of fire and has great **physical strength**. Through the years, there have been many **separate** sightings of Ye Ren. However, the fact that it **actually** exists has never **definitely** been proved.

Scientists would like to capture Ye Ren in the flesh—or at least on film. With that intention, they have made several trips to the jungles of China. Those excursions, however, have not **benefited science** much. So far, footprints eighteen inches long are the only signs anyone has found of the **mysterious** Ye Ren.

Checking Your Reading Power

Put an *x* in the box before the correct answer to each question.

Main Idea
1. This selection is mainly about
   □ a. scientists around the world.
   □ b. villagers in China.
   □ c. Ye Ren.

Supporting Details
2. According to reports, Ye Ren
   □ a. has great strength.
   □ b. has a tail.
   □ c. is afraid of fire.

Vocabulary in Context
3. What is the meaning of the word excursions?
   □ a. sightings
   □ b. trips
   □ c. films

Cause and Effect
4. Scientists have traveled to the jungles of China in order to
   □ a. meet with the leaders of the country.
   □ b. take movies of the countryside.
   □ c. look for Ye Ren.

Inference
5. If there is a Ye Ren, we may infer that it
   □ a. has very small feet.
   □ b. stays hidden most of the time.
   □ c. enjoys meeting people.

More Spelling Power to You

Look back over the boldfaced words in the passage. Pay close attention to how they are spelled. Then, in your notebook, write each word in a sentence and underline the spelling word.

At home, study the spellings of the underlined words. For some good spelling strategies, turn to page 8.

After you have studied the words, you will complete the spelling check on the next page. It contains some words from previous lessons, as well as most of the words from this lesson. So be sure to review all the words you have learned so far in this book. Concentrate especially on the list of words you have misspelled on previous spelling checks.

Checking Your Spelling Power

Complete this exercise without looking back at the words. Each of the sentences below contains one misspelled word. Underline the misspelled word. Then write it correctly on the line before the sentence.

.... 1. The first time I went ice-skating, I felt a bit awkward, but after a while it was actualy quite pleasant.

.... 2. Although everyone appreciated your help, Glen certainly benefitted most from your assistance.

.... 3. Do you believe that a daily program of phisical fitness is really important?

.... 4. The polar bear has great strenth and can move swiftly when the occasion demands it.

.... 5. We became conscious of the fact that the cat had a mysterious smile on its face, and that the canary, evidentally, was missing.

.... 6. The excitement in the air was definitly noticeable.

.... 7. Do not despair; the problem will eventually be solved by sience.

.... 8. When they were younger they were almost always together, but now they have gone their seperate ways.

.... 9. The newspaper report refered to her as "a courageous person."

.... 10. When you do not posess good health, you recognize its importance.

Check your answers in the answer key on page 101. In your notebook, keep a list of the words you misspelled. Study those words until you master them.

Words Often Confused and Misused

The words *right* and *write* are frequently confused and misused. Carefully study the meanings of the words and the sample sentences. Then do the exercise that follows.

right The word *right* means "correct or good." It may also mean "the direction that is opposite of left."

write The word *write* means "to form words or letters, usually with a pencil or pen."

You were **right** to turn **right** at the corner.
How many plays did Shakespeare **write**?
You will not be able to **write** to me if you do not have the **right** address.

Complete the sentences below by writing *right* and *write* in the proper blanks.

1. Please .... once a week, so that we know you're all ....

2. After you figure out the .... answer, ... the solution in the box on the ....

3. When you .... to your senator, carefully explain why you think you are ....

Now review the Words Often Confused and Misused from lessons 1–24. They will be included in the Cumulative Review that begins on the next page.

•Cumulative Review of Units 1-6•

I• In each of the following groups of words, one word is misspelled. Circle the misspelled word. Then write the word correctly on the line to the left.

1. hurryng
   science
   describe

2. recieve
   possess
   scene

3. eighth
   often
   pursuade

4. again
   bigest
   planned

5. refered
   evidently
   committed

6. accurate
   boundery
   anxious

7. argue
   handkerchief
   anounces

8. continually
   ignorant
   acommodate

9. disappear
   indian
   weigh

10. busness
    strength
    brilliant

II• Fill in the blanks in the words to create words that are spelled correctly. Then write the words on the lines to the left.

1. d_vided
2. democra_y
3. assist_nce
4. satisfact_ry
5. sens_ble
6. sp_ _ch
7. experi_n_e
8. sep_r_te
9. criti_i_m
10. ind_p_nd_nt

III• The letters *ie* or *ei* are missing from each of the words below. Fill in the blanks in each word to spell the word correctly. Then write the word on the line to the left.

1. th_ _f
2. y_ _ld
3. w_ _rd
4. gr_ _ve
5. for_ _gn

IV• In each of the following sentences, one of the three underlined words is misspelled. Circle the misspelled word. Then write the word correctly on the line before the sentence.

1. I sincerly enjoy picnicking on a pleasant day.

2. At the beginning of the book, the author states her reasons for writting the novel.

3. The captain asked, "Who was responsable for carrying out the mission?"

75

4. The balloon began to discend slowly, and finally dropped into the ocean.

5. Do you have an explanation for that mysterious occurence?

6. I shall always be gratefull for the college education that has benefited me so much.

7. When we heard that you were coming to town, we immediatly made plans to visit.

8. James will succeed as a comic because his humerous style is really delightful.

9. Somehow, he was able to persuade an aquaintance to take part in his silly scheme.

10. Good literature can actually make an imagnary world seem real.

V• Each of the following sentences contains two words in parentheses. Underline the one that makes the sentence correct. Then write the word on the line to the left.

1. We were just talking about how quickly the summer (past, passed).

2. Henry Clay once said, "I would rather be (right, write) than be president."

3. He found it easier to (accept, except) praise than responsibility.

4. The insurance company did not consider the accident (miner, minor).

5. Just hours after they were (shone, shown) the house, they decided to buy it.

6. In a famous play, Polonius offers his son some (advice, advise).

7. If you (loose, lose) your way, blow this whistle and we'll find you.

8. It's not a question of the *money* involved; it's a matter of (principal, principle).

9. The three wise monkeys could (hear, here) no evil, see no evil, and speak no evil.

10. Do you know (whose, who's) twenty dollar bill this is?

11. It is often a good idea to (right, write) about people and things you know best.

12. Perhaps I'll have another (peace, piece) of pie after all.

13. The lessons of the (past, passed) can help us in the future.

14. I hope that my (knew, new) friends will be my old friends one day.

15. I'm doing well on this exercise; I hope (your, you're) doing well too.

UNIT 7
Olympic Feats

When you have completed this unit, you will have mastered 280 of the words that are most frequently misspelled and 58 words that are commonly confused and misused.

•25•

Amateur athletes from around the globe gather in a **different** country every four years to participate in the Olympic Games. The purpose of the Games is to give athletes an **opportunity** to compete with each other in the spirit of friendship and peace. Each **athlete** knows that it is an honor, as well as a responsibility, to be a **representative** of his or her country.

During ceremonies that **precede** the Games, the participants **pledge obedience** to the rules of sportsmanship and fair play. Then they strive to do their best.

Actually, the Olympic Games are divided into two parts. There are the Summer Games and the Winter Games. The Summer Olympics feature track and field events, while the Winter Olympics highlight **skiing** and skating. Some other Olympic sports are boxing, wrestling, hockey, **swimming**, and high-speed **bicycle** racing.

Checking Your Reading Power

Put an *x* in the box before the correct answer to each question.

Main Idea
1. This selection is mainly about
   - ☐ a. the Summer Olympics.
   - ☐ b. ceremonies at the Olympics.
   - ☐ c. the Olympic Games.

Supporting Details
2. The Olympic Games are held
   - ☐ a. every two years.
   - ☐ b. every four years.
   - ☐ c. in a different country every year.

Vocabulary in Context
3. As used in this selection, what is the meaning of the word highlight?
   - ☐ a. shadow or shade
   - ☐ b. slip or fall
   - ☐ c. feature or spotlight

Cause and Effect
4. Which sentence best explains why the Games are held?
   - ☐ a. The Games give athletes a chance to become rich and famous.
   - ☐ b. The Games give athletes a chance to compete in an atmosphere of friendship and fair play.
   - ☐ c. The Games give athletes a chance to travel around the globe.

Inference
5. We may infer that the Winter Olympics must be held in a country that
   - ☐ a. has ski slopes.
   - ☐ b. is very warm.
   - ☐ c. has the best skiers.

More Spelling Power to You

Look back over the boldfaced words in the passage. Pay close attention to how they are spelled. Then, in your notebook, write each word in a sentence and underline the spelling word.

At home, study the spellings of the underlined words. For some good spelling strategies, turn to page 8.

After you have studied the words, you will complete the spelling check on the next page. It contains some words from previous lessons, as well as most of the words from this lesson. So be sure to review all the words you have learned so far in this book. Concentrate especially on the list of words you misspelled on previous spelling checks.

Checking Your Spelling Power

Complete this exercise without looking back at the words. In each of the following groups of words, one of the words is misspelled. On the line to the left, write the letter of the misspelled word.

1. _____ a. swiming   b. running   c. million
2. _____ a. pledge   b. sieze   c. almost
3. _____ a. remember   b. interrupt   c. preceed
4. _____ a. flys   b. skiing   c. definitely
5. _____ a. character   b. athalete   c. thoroughly
6. _____ a. bycycle   b. individual   c. eleventh
7. _____ a. absolutely   b. obediance   c. physical
8. _____ a. representative b. drownd   c. privilege
9. _____ a. diffrent   b. marriage   c. attempt
10. _____ a. transferred b. realize   c. oportunity

Check your answers in the answer key on page 102. In your notebook, keep a list of the words you misspelled. Study those words until you master them.

Words Often Confused and Misused

The words *desert* and *dessert* are commonly confused and misused. Carefully study the meanings of the words and the sample sentences. Then do the exercise that follows.

desert The noun *desert* (DEZ-ert) means "a dry area or region." The verb *desert* (dih-ZERT) means "to abandon or leave."

dessert The noun *dessert* (dih-ZERT) means "the last course at a meal." (Some people say that you add a second *s* because you always want *more* dessert.)

Fortunately, their guide did not **desert** them in the middle of the **desert**.
He ate so much of the main course that he could barely touch his **dessert**.
She decided to **desert** her diet and order **dessert**.

Complete the sentences below by writing *desert* and *dessert* in the proper blanks.

1. At the edge of the _____ was a store where you could buy sandwiches and _____ .
2. Nothing is as refreshing as a cool _____ in the blazing _____ .
3. He planned to _____ his family and go off to live alone in the _____ .

Now review the Words Often Confused and Misused from previous lessons. They will be included in the Cumulative Review that follows lesson 32.

•26•

Who would have thought that a girl who could not walk as a child would **develop** into a world-class runner?

When she was only four years old, Wilma Rudolph was <u>stricken</u> with a terrible disease. She lost the use of one leg, and doctors could not **guarantee** that she would ever walk again. After a **siege** of more than three years, young Wilma was **finally** able to walk properly.

Wilma began to **exercise** regularly. She also participated in sports as often as **possible**. One day while she was playing basketball in high school, a coach noticed that Wilma could run like **lightning**. He suggested that she take up track, so she did, with amazing **success**.

Before long, Wilma was a star. In the 1960 Olympics, at the age of twenty, she won three gold medals—the most any American woman had ever won in track. Because of her talent and **shining** personality, no one could please a **crowd** the way Wilma Rudolph could.

○ Checking Your Reading Power ○

Put an *x* in the box before the correct answer to each question.

Main Idea
1. This selection is mainly about
   - ☐ a. the life of Wilma Rudolph.
   - ☐ b. why Wilma Rudolph played basketball.
   - ☐ c. a disease that struck Wilma Rudolph.

Supporting Details
2. In the 1960 Olympics, Wilma Rudolph
   - ☐ a. won a total of two events.
   - ☐ b. won three gold medals.
   - ☐ c. was not liked by the fans.

Vocabulary in Context
3. What is the meaning of the word <u>stricken</u>?
   - ☐ a. hit
   - ☐ b. pleased
   - ☐ c. drowned

Cause and Effect
4. Wilma Rudolph took up track because
   - ☐ a. a coach suggested that she try it.
   - ☐ b. her family thought she might win some medals.
   - ☐ c. her friends said she could run like lightning.

Inference
5. This story suggests that
   - ☐ a. Wilma Rudolph was the world's greatest athlete.
   - ☐ b. Wilma's disease was not serious.
   - ☐ c. it is sometimes possible to turn a weakness into a strength.

○ More Spelling Power to You ○

Look back over the boldfaced words in the passage. Pay close attention to how they are spelled. Then, in your notebook, write each word in a sentence and underline the spelling word.

At home, study the spellings of the underlined words. For some good spelling strategies, turn to page 8.

After you have studied the words, you will complete the spelling check on the next page. It contains some words from previous lessons, as well as most of the words from this lesson. So be sure to review all the words you have learned so far in this book. Concentrate especially on the list of words you misspelled on previous spelling checks.

Checking Your Spelling Power

Complete this exercise without looking back at the words. In each of the following pairs of words, one word is spelled incorrectly. Circle that word. Then write it correctly on the line to the left.

.... 1. croud
                different

.... 2. swimming
                possable

.... 3. ansered
                siege

.... 4. shinning
                ancient

.... 5. success
                speek

.... 6. sking
                lightning

.... 7. exercize
                achieve

.... 8. guarante
                athlete

.... 9. finaly
                bicycle

.... 10. precede
                develope

Check your answers in the answer key on page 102. In your notebook, keep a list of the words you misspelled. Study those words until you master them.

Words Often Confused and Misused

The words *their, they're* and *there* are among the most commonly confused and misused words in the English language. However, you can easily learn when to use each word. Carefully study the meanings of the words and the sample sentences. Then do the exercise that follows. Remember that *their* and *they're* are like *its* and *it's, whose* and *who's,* and *your* and *you're.* One word shows possession while the other is a contraction.

their   The word *their* is a possessive pronoun meaning "belonging to them."

they're The word *they're* is a contraction. It means "they are." The apostrophe takes the place of the *a* in *are.*

there   The word *there* means "at or in that place."

The birds flew into **their** nest.
Remind the twins that if **they're** late they will miss the first act.
If you get **there** early, please wait for me.

Complete the sentences below by writing *their, they're* and *there* in the proper blanks.

1. Cats almost always land on .... feet; I think .... amazing.

2. Although .... the best batters on the team, ... always out early, practicing .... hitting.

3. We'll be .... at two o'clock sharp, so please make certain that .... ready.

Now review the Words Often Confused and Misused from previous lessons. They will be included in the Cumulative Review following lesson 32.

•27•

The star of the 1912 Olympics was a twenty-four-year-old American Indian named Jim Thorpe. A **fierce** competitor, with blazing speed and raw power, Thorpe won the five-event pentathlon and the ten-event decathlon—an unbelievable **accomplishment**.

Ten years later, however, a **special committee** determined that Thorpe had not been **eligible** to participate in the Olympic Games. The committee **decided** that Thorpe had been a professional athlete rather than an amateur because he had been given a small sum of **expense** money to play baseball one summer. After much **discussion**, Thorpe was stripped of his Olympic medals. His name was taken out of the Olympic record books, and his victories were also deleted.

More than fifty years later, however, the **decision** was reversed. Thorpe's medals were returned to his family, and his great feats, **omitted** for so long, are now once again part of the Olympic record.

Checking Your Reading Power

Put an *x* in the box before the correct answer to each question.

Main Idea
1. This selection is mainly about
   - ☐ a. the 1912 Olympics.
   - ☐ b. Jim Thorpe's place in Olympic history.
   - ☐ c. the family of a great Olympic athlete.

Supporting Details
2. Which one of the following statements is true?
   - ☐ a. Jim Thorpe did not participate in the 1912 Olympics because he was not eligible.
   - ☐ b. Jim Thorpe won the pentathlon and the decathlon in the 1912 Olympics.
   - ☐ c. At the time of the 1912 Olympics, Jim Thorpe was twenty-eight years old.

Vocabulary in Context
3. What is the meaning of the word deleted?
   - ☐ a. put in
   - ☐ b. taken out
   - ☐ c. questioned

Cause and Effect
4. Jim Thorpe lost his Olympic medals
   - ☐ a. as the result of a committee's decision.
   - ☐ b. because it was discovered that he had not finished first in some events.
   - ☐ c. because of poor sportsmanship on his part.

Inference
5. We may infer that the Olympic Games are open to
   - ☐ a. anyone who wishes to enter.
   - ☐ b. professional athletes only.
   - ☐ c. amateur athletes only.

More Spelling Power to You

Look back over the boldfaced words in the passage. Pay close attention to how they are spelled. Then, in your notebook, write each word in a sentence and underline the spelling word.

At home, study the spellings of the underlined words. For some spelling strategies, turn to page 8.

After you have studied the words, you will complete the spelling check on the next page. It contains some words from previous lessons, as well as most of the words from this lesson. So be sure to review all the words you have learned so far in this book. Concentrate especially on the list of words you misspelled on previous spelling checks.

Checking Your Spelling Power

Complete this exercise without looking back at the words. In each of the following groups of words, one word is misspelled. Circle the misspelled word. Then write it correctly on the line to the left.

....	1. special	sucess	opportunity	unusual
....	2. comittee	crowd	among	forward
....	3. finally	dicided	complete	amusing
....	4. guarantee	really	relief	elegible
....	5. possible	conscience	acomplishment	schedule
....	6. omited	skiing	noticeable	vacant
....	7. fierce	aquire	against	immediately
....	8. representitive	expense	generally	approach
....	9. lieutenant	studying	develop	discusion
....	10. exercise	system	dicision	siege

Check your answers in the answer key on page 102. In your notebook, keep a list of the words you misspelled. Study those words until you master them.

Words Often Confused and Misused

The words *coarse* and *course* are frequently confused and misused. Carefully study the meanings of the words and the sample sentences. Then do the exercise that follows.

coarse The word *coarse* means "rough or crude."

course The word *course* has several meanings. The most common are "a unit of study," "a path," and "part of a meal."

Although his manner seems **coarse**, he is actually quite gentle.
Sandra took an excellent **course** in auto repairs.
The golf ball hit some **coarse** sand and rolled off **course**.

Complete the sentences below by writing *coarse* and *course* in the proper blanks.

1. The man in the .... wool sweater teaches this ....
2. The waiter's manner was so .... we complained after he served the first ....
3. She was removed from the .... because of her .... language.

Now review the Words Often Confused and Misused from previous lessons. They will be included in the Cumulative Review following lesson 32.

•28•

Among people who follow sports, there is general **acknowledgment** that Babe Didrikson Zaharias was America's greatest woman athlete. During her twenty-year career, there seemed to be no **ceiling** on her athletic ability. Indeed, it would be hard to **exaggerate** what she **meant** to sports.

As an all-round athlete, Babe had no **parallel**. Born Mildred Ella Didrikson, classmates used to **address** her as "Babe" because she could smash a baseball "like Babe Ruth." Babe was **built** slender and tall. She was a famous women's professional basketball player for years. She was also renowned as a track-and-field star.

In the 1932 Olympics, Babe won gold medals in the javelin throw and the 80-meter hurdles. She also won a silver medal in the high jump. A few years later, a **mischievous** rival suggested that Babe take up a new sport—golf—in her **leisure** time. Babe did, and she did not **disappoint** her fans. Before she retired, she had won more golf tournaments than any woman who ever lived.

Checking Your Reading Power

Put an *x* in the box before the correct answer to each question.

Main Idea
1. This selection is mainly about
   - ☐ a. the person many people think of as America's greatest woman athlete.
   - ☐ b. some sports played in the 1932 Olympic Games.
   - ☐ c. how to become a champion at golf.

Supporting Details
2. According to this selection, Babe Didrikson
   - ☐ a. was an outstanding swimmer.
   - ☐ b. played professional baseball.
   - ☐ c. played professional basketball.

Vocabulary in Context
3. What is the meaning of the word renowned?
   - ☐ a. new
   - ☐ b. famous
   - ☐ c. swift

Cause and Effect
4. Babe Didrikson was called "Babe" because
   - ☐ a. she asked her classmates to call her by that name.
   - ☐ b. she could hit a baseball like Babe Ruth.
   - ☐ c. her family liked the name.

Inference
5. If Babe had played tennis, she would probably have
   - ☐ a. played poorly.
   - ☐ b. become an outstanding player.
   - ☐ c. disliked the sport.

More Spelling Power to You

Look back over the boldfaced words in the passage. Pay close attention to how they are spelled. Then, in your notebook, write each word in a sentence and underline the spelling word.

At home, study the spellings of the underlined words. For some good spelling strategies, turn to page 8.

After you have studied the words, you will complete the spelling check on the next page. It contains some words from previous lessons, as well as most of the words from this lesson. So be sure to review all the words you have learned so far in this book. Concentrate especially on the list of words you have misspelled on previous spelling checks.

Checking Your Spelling Power

Complete this exercise without looking back at the words. Each of the sentences below contains one misspelled word. Underline the misspelled word. Then write it correctly on the line before the sentence.

.... 1. After much discussion, they decided to paint the cieling blue.

.... 2. The committee did excellent work; however, you should not exagerate its importance.

.... 3. I meant to thank you for going to such great expence, but in the excitement I forgot.

.... 4. His mischievious manner will probably get him into trouble occasionally.

.... 5. Roberta's main accomplishment was the beautiful art work she did in her liesure time.

.... 6. Every athlete, naturally, hopes not to disapoint the fans.

.... 7. I am familiar with both roads; they are paralell to each other and are approximately five miles apart.

.... 8. The house was built without windows; therfore it is not possible for the sun to shine in.

.... 9. When you adress the crowd, it is necessary to speak in a loud voice.

.... 10. We were glad to see you finally receive the aknowledgment you deserve.

Check your answers in the answer key on page 102. In your notebook, keep a list of the words you misspelled. Study those words until you master them.

Words Often Confused and Misused

The words *know* and *no* are sometimes confused and misused. Carefully study the meanings of the words and the sample sentences. Then do the exercise that follows.

know   The word *know* means "to have knowledge or facts."

no   The word *no* means "not at all," or "not any."

Do you **know** how many moons Jupiter has?
I am sorry to have to say **no** to your request.
Mr. Leung is **no** longer here; I do not **know** his new address.

Complete the sentences below by writing *know* and *no* in the proper blanks.

1. Since Andrea is .... better, her mother does not .... when she will be able to return to school.

2. I do not .... if we can make a substitution, because we have .... time-outs left.

3. There is .... way I will be able to .... all the information by tomorrow.

Now review the Words Often Confused and Misused from previous lessons. They will be included in the Cumulative Review following lesson 32.

UNIT 8
Safety First

When you have completed this unit, you will have mastered 320 of the words that are most frequently misspelled and 66 words that are commonly confused and misused.

•29•

Do you know that the kitchen is probably the most **dangerous** room in your house? According to surveys, more **serious** injuries occur there than anywhere else in the home.

Here are a few tips that experts on **safety recommend** to help you **guard** against accidents in the kitchen. First, water and electricity don't mix. Therefore, it is <u>imperative</u> that you keep electrical appliances from getting wet. It is also important to keep napkins and papers off the stove and to turn the handles of pots and pans on the stove inward.

Make sure that **knife** blades are well sharpened. A dull knife is more **likely** to slip and to cause injury. When using a knife, cut away from yourself rather than toward yourself. And don't use water to try to put out an oil or a grease fire. Water will only spread the flames.

Here is one last **suggestion**: Keep a fire extinguisher handy. But if a fire gets out of **control**, do not **endeavor** to combat it. Leave at once and get help.

Checking Your Reading Power

Put an *x* in the box before the correct answer to each question.

Main Idea
1. This selection is mainly about
   - ☐ a. how to prevent accidents in the kitchen.
   - ☐ b. why a dull knife is likely to cause an injury.
   - ☐ c. how to respond to an emergency.

Supporting Details
2. According to the passage, if a fire gets out of control you should
   - ☐ a. try to fight it.
   - ☐ b. go to another room.
   - ☐ c. leave at once.

Vocabulary in Context
3. As used in this selection, the word <u>imperative</u> means
   - ☐ a. very important.
   - ☐ b. not necessary.
   - ☐ c. quite funny.

Cause and Effect
4. Throwing water on a grease fire will
   - ☐ a. put out the fire at once.
   - ☐ b. put out the fire after a while.
   - ☐ c. spread the flames.

Inference
5. Why is it a good idea to turn the handles of pots and pans on the stove inward?
   - ☐ a. Foods cook better that way.
   - ☐ b. They are less likely to be knocked into.
   - ☐ c. You will have more room on the stove.

More Spelling Power to You

Look back over the boldfaced words in the passage. Pay close attention to how they are spelled. Then, in your notebook, write each word in a sentence and underline the spelling word.

At home, study the spellings of the underlined words. For some spelling strategies, turn to page 8.

After you have studied the words, you will complete the spelling check on the next page. It contains some words from previous lessons, as well as most of the words from this lesson. So be sure to review all the words you have learned so far in this book. Concentrate especially on the list of words you misspelled on previous spelling checks.

Checking Your Spelling Power

Complete this exercise without looking back at the words. In each of the following groups of words, one of the words is misspelled. On the line to the left, write the letter of the misspelled word.

1. _____ a. omitted   b. safty   c. address
2. _____ a. likly   b. eligible   c. accidentally
3. _____ a. ceiling   b. exceed   c. sugestion
4. _____ a. guard   b. chief   c. feirce
5. _____ a. exaggerate   b. controll   c. bicycle
6. _____ a. serious   b. bilt   c. restaurant
7. _____ a. parallel   b. ambition   c. dangerus
8. _____ a. recomend   b. mischievous c. having
9. _____ a. seige   b. knife   c. neither
10. _____ a. leisure   b. opinion   c. endevor

Check your answers in the answer key on page 102. In your notebook, keep a list of the words you misspelled. Study those words until you master them.

Words Often Confused and Misused

Because they sound alike and sometimes have similar meanings, the words *capital* and *capitol* are often confused and misused. Carefully study the meanings of the words and the sample sentences. Then do the exercise that follows.

capital   The word *capital* means "a place where a seat of government is located." Sentences and proper names also begin with *capital* letters.

capitol   The word *capitol* means "a government building in which the legislature of a state or country meets."

Paris, the **capital** of France, begins with a **capital** letter.
The roof of the **capitol** is made of marble.
In Albany, the **capital** of New York, we met with a senator in the halls of the **capitol**.

Complete the sentences below by writing *capital* and *capitol* in the proper blanks.

1. When Ruth was in Sacramento, the _____ of California, she had lunch in the cafeteria at the _____ .

2. Washington, D.C., the _____ of the United States, must always be written with a _____ letter.

3. The _____ is in the center of the city; it is the most striking building in the _____ .

Now review the Words Often Confused and Misused from previous lessons. They will be included in the Cumulative Review following lesson 32.

• 30 •

Seat belts save lives. According to a **government bulletin**, if every driver and passenger buckled up, more than five thousand traffic deaths would be prevented each year.

Still, some people refuse to wear seat belts. What is the reason for their **prejudice** against seat belts?

A common excuse is that seat belts are not **comfortable**—that they are a **hindrance** to movement. Of course, broken bones are far more uncomfortable, and you can't move at all when you are in a **cemetery**.

Some people offer the **argument** that it is safer to be thrown from the car in the event of a crash. People who believe that **deceive** themselves. Being thrown from a car is twenty-five times more lethal than being held in place by a seat belt.

So the next time you are in an auto, use your **intelligence** and **knowledge**. Buckle up! Seat belts are good for your health.

Checking Your Reading Power

Put an *x* in the box before the correct answer to each question.

Main Idea
1. This selection is mainly about
   - ☐ a. a government bulletin.
   - ☐ b. an argument against buckling up.
   - ☐ c. the importance of wearing a seat belt.

Supporting Details
2. Being thrown from a car in a crash is
   - ☐ a. about as dangerous as being held in the car by a seat belt.
   - ☐ b. less dangerous than being held in the car by a seat belt.
   - ☐ c. much more dangerous than being held in the car by a seat belt.

Vocabulary in Context
3. What is the meaning of the word lethal?
   - ☐ a. upsetting
   - ☐ b. deadly
   - ☐ c. restricting

Cause and Effect
4. If all drivers and passengers wore seat belts,
   - ☐ a. thousands of lives would be saved each year.
   - ☐ b. there would be many more traffic deaths each year.
   - ☐ c. the number of traffic deaths would remain about the same.

Inference
5. Some people say that wearing seat belts is uncomfortable. The passage suggests that this argument is
   - ☐ a. excellent.
   - ☐ b. foolish.
   - ☐ c. wise.

More Spelling Power to You

Look back over the boldfaced words in the passage. Pay close attention to how they are spelled. Then, in your notebook, write each word in a sentence and underline the spelling word.

At home, study the spellings of the underlined words. For some spelling strategies, turn to page 8.

After you have studied the words, you will complete the spelling check on the next page. It contains some words from previous lessons, as well as most of the words from this lesson. So be sure to review all the words you have learned so far in this book. Concentrate especially on the list of words you misspelled on previous spelling checks.

Checking Your Spelling Power

Complete this exercise without looking back at the words. In each of the following pairs of words, one word is spelled incorrectly. Circle that word. Then write it correctly on the line to the left.

....	1. knowledge serius	....	6. hinderance control
....	2. comftable cafeteria	....	7. suggestion cemetary
....	3. arguement pledge	....	8. intellagence dependent
....	4. different goverment	....	9. predjudice disappoint
....	5. decieve recommend	....	10. acknowledgment buletin

Check your answers in the answer key on page 102. In your notebook, keep a list of the words you misspelled. Study those words until you master them.

Words Often Confused and Misused

The words *choose* and *chose* are commonly confused and misused. Carefully study the meanings of the words and the sample sentences. Then do the exercise that follows.

choose   The word *choose* means "select or pick." Notice that *choose* shows either the present or the future tense.

chose   The word *chose* means "selected or picked." *Chose* is the past tense of *choose*.

> Please **choose** your partner for the dance.
> Yesterday we **chose** Manuela as treasurer.
> My sister, Diane, didn't know which college to **choose**; finally she **chose** State University.

Complete the sentences below by writing *choose* and *chose* in the proper blanks.

1. I'm glad I .... this gift; which gift do you plan to .... ?
2. Forced to .... between baseball and football, Mark eventually .... baseball.
3. If you are still unhappy with the book you ...., you may .... another.

Now review the Words Often Confused and Misused from previous lessons. They will be included in the Cumulative Review following lesson 32.

• 31 •

Noise, **particularly** loud noise, can be harmful to your health. Studies have shown that too much loud noise makes people angry, <u>irritable</u> and **tired**. It can also cause headaches, stomachaches, and many other illnesses. In **laboratory** experiments, for example, monkeys developed high blood pressure after being exposed to months of loud noise.

Today, about twenty million Americans suffer from hearing loss. In the majority of cases, loud noise is the **villain**. Therefore, you might want to lower the volume on those headphones that look so **innocent**. After all, you don't want to **sacrifice** your hearing for the sake of a rock band, no matter how great its **rhythm**. And the next time you see someone sitting right next to a radio or stereo that is blaring away, **perhaps** you could explain in a **courteous** way that loud noise is **guilty** of contributing to poor health.

Checking Your Reading Power

Put an *x* in the box before the correct answer to each question.

Main Idea
1. This selection is mainly about
   - ☐ a. studies made by experts on health.
   - ☐ b. the ways in which loud noises can be harmful.
   - ☐ c. why headphones are dangerous.

Supporting Details
2. According to the selection, monkeys exposed to loud noise developed
   - ☐ a. headaches.
   - ☐ b. stomachaches.
   - ☐ c. high blood pressure.

Vocabulary in Context
3. Judging from the context of the sentence in which it appears, what is the meaning of the word <u>irritable</u>?
   - ☐ a. angry
   - ☐ b. happy
   - ☐ c. calm

Cause and Effect
4. Loud noise causes some people to
   - ☐ a. feel energized.
   - ☐ b. become nervous.
   - ☐ c. hear better.

Inference
5. This article suggests that you should
   - ☐ a. sit right next to a radio or a stereo when you are listening to music.
   - ☐ b. be careful when using headphones.
   - ☐ c. encourage friends to listen to classical music.

More Spelling Power to You

Look back over the boldfaced words in the passage. Pay close attention to how they are spelled. Then, in your notebook, write each word in a sentence and underline the spelling word.

At home, study the spellings of the underlined words. For some good spelling strategies, turn to page 8.

After you have studied the words, you will complete the spelling check on the next page. It contains some words from previous lessons, as well as most of the words from this lesson. So be sure to review all the words you have learned so far in this book. Concentrate especially on the list of words you misspelled on previous spelling checks.

Checking Your Spelling Power

Complete this exercise without looking back at the words. In each of the following groups of words, one word is misspelled. Circle the misspelled word. Then write it correctly on the line to the left.

....	1. government	guard	terrible	inocent
....	2. tired	knive	intelligence	likely
....	3. labratory	hindrance	dangerous	disagreeable
....	4. bulletin	fortunately	rythm	special
....	5. cemetery	gilty	swimming	preferred
....	6. purhaps	prejudice	committee	hesitate
....	7. permanent	meant	sacrafice	endeavor
....	8. parallel	unnecessary	shriek	villian
....	9. comfortable	paticularly	preparation	expense
....	10. argument	quantity	courtious	sufficient

Check your answers in the answer key on page 102. In your notebook, keep a list of the words you misspelled. Study those words until you master them.

Words Often Confused and Misused

The words *plain* and *plane* are frequently confused and misused. Carefully study the meanings of the words and the sample sentences. Then do the exercise that follows.

plain   The word *plain* means "simple or easy." It may also refer to "a prairie, or flat and level piece of land."

plane   The word *plane* has several meanings. The most common are "an airplane" and "a tool used for smoothing or shaping wood."

The pioneers who lived on the **plain** were used to eating **plain** meals.
In wood shop, Gwen used a **plane** to smooth the wings of the **plane** she had built.
The **plane** flew high above the **plain**.

Complete the sentences below by writing *plain* and *plane* in the proper blanks.

1. The carpenter always wore a .... apron to keep the shavings from the

   .... away from his clothing.

2. Looking down from the ...., we could clearly see the outlines of a large, green

   ....

3. The pilot used clear, ... language to discuss the teamwork necessary to fly a

   large jet ....

Now review the Words Often Confused and Misused from previous lessons. They will be included in the Cumulative Review following lesson 32.

•32•

One should never travel in the desert without plenty of water. Several years ago, two young men **practically** lost their lives when they forgot that rule of safety.

Their problems began when their car got stuck in the soft sand of the Mojave Desert. Since the auto **stopped** just a short distance away from a hard gravel road, they began to push the car, **hoping** to reach the road.

The sun, however, blazed down with a **vengeance**, creating an **awful** heat. One man passed out and the other grew dizzy. Luckily, however, the second man had an idea. He drained some water from the car's radiator and drank the precious liquid. Repeating the **procedure**, he obtained some water for his **friend**. The water made the **difference**. Once refreshed, they had enough strength to get the car onto the road. After several **tries** at starting the car, the men got the motor to turn over, and they continued their journey.

In **summary**: one should always take along a generous supply of water when traveling in the desert.

Checking Your Reading Power

Put an *x* in the box before the correct answer to each question.

Main Idea
1. This selection is mainly about
   - ☐ a. why a car got stuck in the desert.
   - ☐ b. several rules of safety to follow when traveling.
   - ☐ c. how water saved the lives of two men in the desert.

Supporting Details
2. The car came to a halt
   - ☐ a. not far from a road.
   - ☐ b. many miles from a road.
   - ☐ c. on a hard gravel road.

Vocabulary in Context
3. What is the meaning of the word refreshed?
   - ☐ a. to exhaust or make tired
   - ☐ b. to make fresh again
   - ☐ c. to cause sadness or sorrow

Cause and Effect
4. One man passed out because he
   - ☐ a. was hungry.
   - ☐ b. had been ill.
   - ☐ c. couldn't take the heat.

Inference
5. The car's motor probably didn't turn over right away because
   - ☐ a. the car was almost out of gas.
   - ☐ b. it was a very old car.
   - ☐ c. the car was very hot.

More Spelling Power to You

Look back over the boldfaced words in the passage. Pay close attention to how they are spelled. Then, in your notebook, write each word in a sentence and underline the spelling word.

At home, study the spellings of the underlined words. For some good spelling strategies, turn to page 8.

After you have studied the words, you will complete the spelling check on the next page. It contains some words from previous lessons, as well as most of the words from this lesson. So be sure to review all the words you have learned so far in this book. Concentrate especially on the list of words you have misspelled on previous spelling checks.

Checking Your Spelling Power

Complete this exercise without looking back at the words. Each of the sentences below contains one misspelled word. Underline the misspelled word. Then write it correctly on the line before the sentence.

       1. A frend is someone who is truly willing to make a sacrifice for you.

       2. One day in his laboratory, Dr. Frankenstein created an awfull and extraordinary creature.

       3. After several tries, we eventually met with the reprasentative.

       4. According to the police, the villain is dangerous and is seeking vengance.

       5. I am hopeing to visit Montreal during Easter vacation, since that city is particularly beautiful in the spring.

       6. If you follow a different proceedure, perhaps you will have better results.

       7. The teacher said, "It is your responsibility to develop a thoughtful sumary."

       8. My heart nearly stoped beating when I heard that you had had a serious accident while skiing.

       9. In the courtroom, practicaly everyone had an opinion about whether the defendant was innocent or guilty.

      10. Let me take this opportunity to offer a suggestion: always remember that you *can* make a diffrence.

Check your answers in the answer key on page 102. In your notebook, keep a list of the words you misspelled. Study those words until you master them.

Words Often Confused and Misused

The words *hole* and *whole* are often confused and misused. Carefully study the meanings of the words and the sample sentences. Then do the exercise that follows.

    hole   The word *hole* means "an open or hollow place."

  whole   The word *whole* means "entire or complete."

       Who first put the **hole** in the middle of the doughnut?
       It was a struggle, but I finished the **whole** meal.
       Mike spent the **whole** day digging a **hole** for the pool.

Complete the sentences below by writing *hole* and *whole* in the proper blanks.

1. Bea missed a _____ week of school after she tripped in a _____ and sprained her ankle.

2. A large _____ in your jacket can ruin your _____ suit.

3. Our lawyer's _____ argument was so strong they could not find a _____ in the case.

Now review the Words Often Confused and Misused from lessons 1–32. They will be included in the Cumulative Review that begins on the next page.

•Cumulative Review of Units 1-8•

I• In each of the following groups of words, one word is misspelled. Circle the misspelled word. Then write the word correctly on the line to the left.

1. biginning
   lightning
   villain

2. government
   liberary
   college

3. shining
   address
   ocurr

4. suprise
   happened
   precede

5. control
   decieve
   stopped

6. procedure
   dissappoint
   sense

7. prejudice
   ommitted
   interesting

8. bulletin
   rhythm
   ocassion

9. writen
   argument
   guard

10. sincerely
    acomodate
    acknowledgment

II• Fill in the blanks in the words to create words that are spelled correctly. Then write the words on the lines to the left.

1. d__spair
2. nonsen__e
3. obedi__nce
4. d__cided
5. p__rsuade
6. sep__r__te
7. cem__t__ry
8. criti__i__m
9. intell__g__n__e
10. r__spons__b__l__ty

III• The letters *ie* or *ei* are missing from each of the words below. Fill in the blanks in each word to spell the word correctly. Then write the word on the line to the left.

1. f____rce
2. dec____ve
3. ach____ve
4. c____ling
5. s____ge

IV• In each of the following sentences, one of the three underlined words is misspelled. Circle the misspelled word. Then write the word correctly on the line before the sentence.

1. It is true that <u>succes</u> is <u>often</u> <u>built</u> on pride and hard work.

2. By law, a person is considered <u>innocent</u> <u>untill</u> proven <u>guilty</u>.

3. Joellyn <u>trys</u> to <u>exercise</u> twenty minutes a day during her <u>leisure</u> time.

4. These heroes were willing to sacrifise their lives for the safety of others.

5. A pleasant and curteous manner can make a difference when you are applying for a job.

6. Can someone, perhaps, attempt to give you the homework during your abcense?

7. The garantee on the equipment covered practically everything.

8. I recommend that you try writing another summary.

9. Her decision was definitely based on knowlege of the facts.

10. Be careful—our mischevous friend is likely to play a trick on us.

V. Each of the following sentences contains two or three words in parentheses. Underline the one that makes the sentence correct. Then write the word on the line to the left.

1. It is hard to put a square peg into a round (hole, whole).

2. Robinson Crusoe lived for years on a (desert, dessert) island.

3. In 1927, Charles Lindbergh flew a (plain, plane) from New York to Paris.

4. Do you (know, no) the correct word for this sentence?

5. A Greek philosopher said, "Of evils we must (choose, chose) the least."

6. Have you ever been to Madrid, the (capital, capitol) of Spain?

7. Every June, our (principal, principle) wishes the graduating class good luck.

8. Beware of tigers when (their, they're, there) hungry.

9. As you learned earlier, snakes have (know, no) ears.

10. You can relax and read a book regardless of the (weather, whether).

11. At the end of the argument, the umpire (threw, through) the player out of the game.

12. According to Shakespeare, "The (coarse, course) of true love never did run smooth."

13. The card said: "Let us all work for world (peace, piece)."

14. My favorite day of the (weak, week) is Friday.

15. There are none so deaf as those who will not (hear, here).

Answer Key

UNIT 1

Lesson 1

Checking Your Reading Power
1.c 2.b 3.b 4.c 5.c

Checking Your Spelling Power
1.c 2.b 3.a 4.b 5.a 6.a 7.c 8.b 9.b 10.c

Words Often Confused and Misused
1. accept/except   2. except/accept   3. accept/except

Lesson 2

Checking Your Reading Power
1.c 2.c 3.a 4.a 5.b

Checking Your Spelling Power
1. approach   2. occasionally   3. drowned   4. biggest
5. truly   6. weigh   7. equipped   8. usually   9. sufficient
10. surprise

Words Often Confused and Misused
1. loose/lose   2. loose/lose   3. loose/lose

Lesson 3

Checking Your Reading Power
1.a 2.b 3.a 4.b 5.a

Checking Your Spelling Power
1. shriek   2. all right   3. awkward   4. nonsense
5. probably   6. flies   7. generally   8. system
9. dependent   10. making

Words Often Confused and Misused
1. threw/through   2. threw/through   3. through/threw

Lesson 4

Checking Your Reading Power
1.c 2.a 3.a 4.c 5.c

Checking Your Spelling Power
1. impossible   2. explanation   3. fascinating   4. grateful
5. ache   6. dependent   7. therefore   8. absolutely
9. believe   10. necessary

Words Often Confused and Misused
1. quiet/quite   2. quite/quiet   3. quite/quiet

UNIT 2

Lesson 5

Checking Your Reading Power
1.c 2.b 3.c 4.c 5.c

Checking Your Spelling Power
1.b 2.c 3.a 4.b 5.a 6.b 7.c 8.a 9.b 10.c

Words Often Confused and Misused
1. it's/its   2. it's/it's   3. its/it's

Lesson 6

Checking Your Reading Power
1.c 2.b 3.c 4.b 5.c

Checking Your Spelling Power
1. describe   2. written   3. balloon   4. receive
5. accidentally   6. relief   7. excitement   8. usually
9. eventually   10. all right

Words Often Confused and Misused
1. whether/weather   2. weather/whether
3. whether/weather

Lesson 7

Checking Your Reading Power
1.c 2.b 3.a 4.a 5.c

Checking Your Spelling Power
1. continually   2. across   3. using   4. conquer   5. forward
6. courageous   7. celebrate   8. preparation   9. accompany
10. occasionally

Words Often Confused and Misused
1. already/all ready   2. all ready/already
3. already/all ready

Lesson 8

Checking Your Reading Power
1.b 2.b 3.a 4.a 5.c

Checking Your Spelling Power
1. attendance   2. succeed   3. familiar   4. extraordinary
5. recognize   6. occasion   7. losing   8. business   9. speak
10. exhibit

Words Often Confused and Misused
1. whose/who's   2. whose/who's   3. who's/whose

Cumulative Review of Units 1 and 2

I. 1. all right   2. equipped   3. eventually   4. forward
   5. drowned   6. approach   7. business   8. generally
   9. accidentally   10. nonsense

II. 1. terrible   2. discover   3. attendance   4. preparation
    5. conquer   6. speak   7. impossible   8. responsible
    9. dependent   10. description

III. 1. receive   2. height   3. relief   4. shriek   5. believe

IV. 1. library   2. fascinating   3. excitement
    4. interesting   5. surprise   6. acquire   7. straight
    8. necessary   9. flies   10. occasion

V. 1. quiet   2. weather   3. already   4. its   5. through
   6. who's   7. accept   8. lose   9. quite   10. threw
   11. it's   12. loose   13. except   14. whose   15. whether

UNIT 3

Lesson 9

Checking Your Reading Power
1.b 2.b 3.c 4.a 5.b

Checking Your Spelling Power
1.c 2.c 3.b 4.a 5.b 6.c 7.b 8.a 9.a 10.b

Words Often Confused and Misused
1. to/too/two   2. to/to/two/too   3. too/to/to/to/two

Lesson 10

Checking Your Reading Power
1.c 2.b 3.a 4.b 5.b

Checking Your Spelling Power
1. always   2. forty   3. awkward   4. succeed
5. extraordinary   6. existence   7. interrupt   8. permitted
9. valuable   10. disagreeable

Words Often Confused and Misused
1. than/then   2. then/than   3. then/than

Lesson 11

Checking Your Reading Power
1.c 2.a 3.c 4.b 5.a

Checking Your Spelling Power
1. cafeteria   2. having   3. similar   4. sandwich   5. prefer
6. naturally   7. million   8. restaurant   9. favorite
10. banquet

Words Often Confused and Misused
1. weak/week   2. week/weak/week   3. weak/week

Lesson 12

Checking Your Reading Power
1.c 2.c 3.a 4.a 5.b

Checking Your Spelling Power
1. eventually   2. appreciate   3. temperature   4. Indian
5. relief   6. extremely   7. ordinary   8. buried   9. before
10. occur

Words Often Confused and Misused
1. you're/your/you're   2. your/your/you're
3. you're/your/your

UNIT 4

Lesson 13

Checking Your Reading Power
1.b 2.a 3.b 4.c 5.b

Checking Your Spelling Power
1.b 2.a 3.a 4.a 5.c 6.b 7.a 8.b 9.a 10.c

Words Often Confused and Misused
1. knew/new/new   2. new/knew   3. knew/new

Lesson 14

Checking Your Reading Power
1.b 2.a 3.a 4.b 5.c

Checking Your Spelling Power
1. vacant   2. twelfth   3. grateful   4. consider   5. preferred
6. surprise   7. occurrence   8. calendar   9. genuine
10. humorous

Words Often Confused and Misused
1. stationary/stationery   2. stationery/stationary
3. stationary/stationery

Lesson 15

Checking Your Reading Power
1.b 2.c 3.a 4.c 5.b

Checking Your Spelling Power
1. hesitate   2. seize   3. argue   4. honorable   5. pursue
6. embarrass   7. responsibility   8. defense   9. occurred
10. exceed

Words Often Confused and Misused
1. altogether/all together   2. all together/altogether
3. altogether/all together

Lesson 16

Checking Your Reading Power
1.c 2.a 3.c 4.a 5.c

Checking Your Spelling Power
1. appearance   2. answered   3. occurred   4. certainly
5. doubt   6. usually   7. apologize   8. accommodate
9. approximately   10. therefore

Words Often Confused and Misused
1. brake/break   2. break/brake   3. brake/break

Cumulative Review of Units 1-4

I. 1. exceed   2. embarrass   3. quantity   4. preferred
    5. humorous   6. criticism   7. opinion   8. dependent
    9. judgment   10. accommodate

II. 1. describe   2. consider   3. appearance   4. existence
    5. excellent   6. apologize   7. cafeteria
    8. approximately   9. permanent   10. responsibility

III. 1. chief   2. neither   3. seize   4. believe   5. weigh

IV. 1. honorable   2. schedule   3. flies   4. until   5. truly
    6. temperature   7. receive   8. speak   9. all right
    10. although

V. 1. new   2. your   3. week   4. than   5. it's   6. too
    7. whether   8. all ready   9. stationery   10. quiet
    11. accept   12. break   13. whose   14. lose
    15. through

UNIT 5

Lesson 17

Checking Your Reading Power
1.c 2.b 3.c 4.a 5.b

Checking Your Spelling Power
1.b 2.b 3.c 4.a 5.a 6.a 7.c 8.b 9.b 10.a

Words Often Confused and Misused
1. hear/here 2. here/hear 3. hear/here

Lesson 18

Checking Your Reading Power
1.b 2.a 3.c 4.a 5.c

Checking Your Spelling Power
1. writing 2. independent 3. paid 4. remember
5. heroes 6. democracy 7. vacuum 8. especially
9. existence 10. absence

Words Often Confused and Misused
1. shone/shown 2. shown/shone 3. shone/shown

Lesson 19

Checking Your Reading Power
1.b 2.b 3.c 4.a 5.b

Checking Your Spelling Power
1. amusing 2. literature 3. author 4. announces
5. conscience 6. fascinating 7. ignorant 8. sensible
9. committed 10. character

Words Often Confused and Misused
1. peace/piece 2. piece/peace 3. piece/peace

Lesson 20

Checking Your Reading Power
1.a 2.c 3.a 4.c 5.b

Checking Your Spelling Power
1. thief 2. marriage 3. despair 4. interesting
5. sincerely 6. disappear 7. beautiful 8. descend
9. grieve 10. judgment

Words Often Confused and Misused
1. advise/advice 2. advise/advice 3. advice/advise

UNIT 6

Lesson 21

Checking Your Reading Power
1.c 2.b 3.b 4.c 5.a

Checking Your Spelling Power
1.b 2.a 3.c 4.a 5.b 6.b 7.b 8.a 9.c 10.b

Words Often Confused and Misused
1. principal/principal 2. principle/principal
3. principal/principle

Lesson 22

Checking Your Reading Power
1.a 2.b 3.a 4.c 5.a

Checking Your Spelling Power
1. ancient 2. divided 3. immediately 4. truly
5. scheme 6. privilege 7. eighth 8. tragedy
9. transferred 10. individual

Words Often Confused and Misused
1. passed/past 2. past/passed 3. past/passed

Lesson 23

Checking Your Reading Power
1.a 2.c 3.b 4.b 5.c

Checking Your Spelling Power
1. really 2. almost 3. captain 4. conscious
5. thoroughly 6. assistance 7. achieve 8. carrying
9. pleasant 10. noticeable

Words Often Confused and Misused
1. miner/minor 2. minor/minor 3. miner/minor

Lesson 24

Checking Your Reading Power
1.c 2.a 3.b 4.c 5.b

Checking Your Spelling Power
1. actually 2. benefited 3. physical 4. strength
5. evidently 6. definitely 7. science 8. separate
9. referred 10. possess

Words Often Confused and Misused
1. write/right 2. right/write/right 3. write/right

Cumulative Review of Units 1-6

I. 1. hurrying 2. receive 3. persuade 4. biggest
    5. referred 6. boundary 7. announces
    8. accommodate 9. Indian 10. business

II. 1. divided 2. democracy 3. assistance
    4. satisfactory 5. sensible 6. speech 7. experience
    8. separate 9. criticism 10. independent

III. 1. thief 2. yield 3. weird 4. grieve 5. foreign

IV. 1. sincerely 2. writing 3. responsible 4. descend
    5. occurrence 6. grateful 7. immediately
    8. humorous 9. acquaintance 10. imaginary

V. 1. passed 2. right 3. accept 4. minor 5. shown
    6. advice 7. lose 8. principle 9. hear 10. whose
    11. write 12. piece 13. past 14. new 15. you're

UNIT 7

Lesson 25

Checking Your Reading Power
1.c 2.b 3.c 4.b 5.a

Checking Your Spelling Power
1.a 2.b 3.c 4.a 5.b 6.a 7.b 8.b 9.a 10.c

Words Often Confused and Misused
1. desert/dessert 2. dessert/desert 3. desert/desert

Lesson 26

Checking Your Reading Power
1.a 2.b 3.a 4.a 5.c

Checking Your Spelling Power
1. crowd 2. possible 3. answered 4. shining 5. speak
6. skiing 7. exercise 8. guarantee 9. finally
10. develop

Words Often Confused and Misused
1. their/they're 2. they're/they're/their 3. there/they're

Lesson 27

Checking Your Reading Power
1.b 2.b 3.b 4.a 5.c

Checking Your Spelling Power
1. success 2. committee 3. decided 4. eligible
5. accomplishment 6. omitted 7. acquire
8. representative 9. discussion 10. decision

Words Often Confused and Misused
1. coarse/course 2. coarse/course 3. course/coarse

Lesson 28

Checking Your Reading Power
1.a 2.c 3.b 4.b 5.b

Checking Your Spelling Power
1. ceiling 2. exaggerate 3. expense 4. mischievous
5. leisure 6. disappoint 7. parallel 8. therefore
9. address 10. acknowledgment

Words Often Confused and Misused
1. no/know 2. know/no 3. no/know

UNIT 8

Lesson 29

Checking Your Reading Power
1.a 2.c 3.a 4.c 5.b

Checking Your Spelling Power
1.b 2.a 3.c 4.c 5.b 6.b 7.c 8.a 9.a 10.c

Words Often Confused and Misused
1. capital/capitol 2. capital/capital 3. capitol/capital

Lesson 30

Checking Your Reading Power
1.c 2.c 3.b 4.a 5.b

Checking Your Spelling Power
1. serious 2. comfortable 3. argument 4. government
5. deceive 6. hindrance 7. cemetery 8. intelligence
9. prejudice 10. bulletin

Words Often Confused and Misused
1. chose/choose 2. choose/chose 3. chose/choose

Lesson 31

Checking Your Reading Power
1.b 2.c 3.a 4.b 5.b

Checking Your Spelling Power
1. innocent 2. knife 3. laboratory 4. rhythm 5. guilty
6. perhaps 7. sacrifice 8. villain 9. particularly
10. courteous

Words Often Confused and Misused
1. plain/plane 2. plane/plain 3. plain/plane

Lesson 32

Checking Your Reading Power
1.c 2.a 3.b 4.c 5.c

Checking Your Spelling Power
1. friend 2. awful 3. representative 4. vengeance
5. hoping 6. procedure 7. summary 8. stopped
9. practically 10. difference

Words Often Confused and Misused
1. whole/hole 2. hole/whole 3. whole/hole

Cumulative Review of Units 1-8

I. 1. beginning 2. library 3. occur 4. surprise
5. deceive 6. disappoint 7. omitted 8. occasion
9. written 10. accommodate

II. 1. despair 2. nonsense 3. obedience 4. decided
5. persuade 6. separate 7. cemetery 8. criticism
9. intelligence 10. responsibility

III. 1. fierce 2. deceive 3. achieve 4. ceiling 5. siege

IV. 1. success 2. until 3. tries 4. sacrifice
5. courteous 6. absence 7. guarantee 8. writing
9. knowledge 10. mischievous

V. 1. hole 2. desert 3. plane 4. know 5. choose
6. capital 7. principal 8. they're 9. no 10. weather
11. threw 12. course 13. peace 14. week 15. hear

•List of Words by Lessons•

Lesson 1	dependent sense accept/except	discover surprise	fascinating truly	making using	receive victim
Lesson 2	although generally loose/lose	approach occasionally	biggest sufficient	drowned usually	equipped weigh
Lesson 3	all right shriek threw/through	awkward straight	flies studying	nonsense system	probably toward
Lesson 4	absolutely impossible quiet/quite	ache necessary	believe terrible	explanation therefore	grateful unusual
Lesson 5	acquire library its/it's	beginning responsible	career succeed	description until	interesting written
Lesson 6	accidentally eventually weather/whether	ambition excitement	balloon happened	busy height	describe relief
Lesson 7	accompany conquer all ready/already	across continually	against courageous	celebrate forward	coming preparation
Lesson 8	attendance familiar whose/who's	brilliant losing	business occasion	exhibit recognize	extraordinary speak
Lesson 9	always quantity to/too/two	criticism salary	importance soldier	often similar	paid valuable
Lesson 10	anxious interrupt than/then	disagreeable million	existence permitted	forty sandwich	guessed source
Lesson 11	among having weak/week	banquet naturally	cafeteria prefer	favorite restaurant	genuine suppose
Lesson 12	appreciate extremely your/you're	around Indian	before occur	buried ordinary	enough temperature
Lesson 13	attempt permanent knew/new	chief proceed	completely schedule	fortunately speech	handkerchief unnecessary
Lesson 14	argue neither stationary/stationery	calendar occurrence	consider preferred	eleventh twelfth	humorous vacant
Lesson 15	apologize honorable all together/altogether	defense occurred	embarrass pursue	exceed responsibility	hesitate seize
Lesson 16	accommodate doubt brake/break	answered excellent	appearance fourth	approximately judgment	certainly opinion

Lesson 17	acquaintance picnicking hear/here	college professor	dropped remember	especially running	hurrying weird
Lesson 18	absence independent shone/shown	author ignorant	democracy realize	foreign vacuum	heroes writing
Lesson 19	achieve conscience peace/piece	amusing literature	announces sensible	character stubborn	committed together
Lesson 20	ancient grieve advice/advise	beautiful marriage	descend persuade	despair sincerely	disappear thief
Lesson 21	accurate experience principal/principle	again imaginary	boundary lieutenant	carrying satisfactory	equipment tragedy
Lesson 22	divided planned past/passed	eighth privilege	heard scene	immediately scheme	individual transferred
Lesson 23	almost noticeable miner/minor	assistance pleasant	captain really	conscious thoroughly	evidently yield
Lesson 24	actually possess right/write	benefited referred	definitely science	mysterious separate	physical strength
Lesson 25	athlete precede desert/dessert	bicycle pledge	different representative	obedience skiing	opportunity swimming
Lesson 26	crowd lightning their/they're/there	develop possible	exercise shining	finally siege	guarantee success
Lesson 27	accomplishment eligible coarse/course	committee expense	decided fierce	decision omitted	discussion special
Lesson 28	acknowledgment exaggerate know/no	address leisure	built meant	ceiling mischievous	disappoint parallel
Lesson 29	control likely capital/capitol	dangerous recommend	endeavor safety	guard serious	knife suggestion
Lesson 30	argument government choose/chose	bulletin hindrance	cemetery intelligence	comfortable knowledge	deceive prejudice
Lesson 31	courteous perhaps plain/plane	guilty rhythm	innocent sacrifice	laboratory tired	particularly villain
Lesson 32	awful procedure hole/whole	difference stopped	friend summary	hoping tries	practically vengeance